NEW DIRECTIONS
FOR TEACHING AND
LEARNING

Number 5 • 1981

NEW DIRECTIONS FOR TEACHING AND LEARNING

A Quarterly Sourcebook
Kenneth E. Eble and John F. Noonan, Editors-in-Chief

Number 5, 1981

The Administrator's Role in Effective Teaching

Alan E. Guskin
Guest Editor

Jossey-Bass Inc., Publishers
San Francisco • Washington • London

THE ADMINISTRATOR'S ROLE IN EFFECTIVE TEACHING
New Directions for Teaching and Learning
Number 5, 1981
  Alan E. Guskin, Guest Editor

New Directions for Teaching and Learning is published quarterly
by Jossey-Bass Inc., Publishers. Subscriptions are available
at the regular rate for institutions, libraries, and agencies
of $30 for one year. Individuals may subscribe at the special
professional rate of $18 for one year.

Correspondence:
Subscriptions, single-issue orders, change of address notices,
undelivered copies, and other correspondence should be sent to
New Directions Subscriptions, Jossey-Bass Inc., Publishers,
433 California Street, San Francisco, California 94104.

Editorial correspondence should be sent to the Editors-in-Chief,
Kenneth E. Eble or John F. Noonan, Center for Improving
Teaching Effectiveness, Virginia Commonwealth University,
Richmond, Virginia 23284.

Library of Congress Catalogue Card Number LC 80-84307
International Standard Serial Number ISSN 0271-0633
International Standard Book Number ISBN 87589-866-1

Cover design by Willi Baum
Manufactured in the United States of America

Contents

Editor's Notes

Facilitating quality teaching is one of the most important functions of university administrators. Yet the relationship between teaching and administration is rarely discussed. The result is that many faculty members and administrators are not as aware as they might be of how each can contribute to increasing the effectiveness of the other in facilitating the teaching/learning process.

An an applied social psychologist and chancellor of a university, I have been interested in the nature of leadership in higher education and in the effect of different styles of leadership on the development of universities. When Ken Eble asked me to edit a sourcebook on the topic of how administrators facilitate the teaching/learning process, I was intrigued with the opportunity to extend my own conceptual analysis of leadership to this relatively unexplored area.

As I thought about the topic and whom I would ask to contribute chapters, I was influenced by a number of recent personal experiences. I had just completed a chapter for another sourcebook (Guskin, 1980) and was impressed with the scarcity of conceptual analysis in the literature on leadership in higher education. There is a great deal written, but most of it is anecdotal rather than analytical. At about the same time, I was asked to conduct two workshops on leadership in universities; one to about thirty academic vice-presidents and another to the senior administrative team of a medium-sized university. In general, I presented the same material I wrote about in my chapter, although the workshop discussion led to further development of the theme. The reaction of the participants impressed on me the desire that these administrators have for some conceptual tools to analyze the situations in which they find themselves.

Most senior university administrators are not trained in disciplines that provide them with conceptual tools for analyzing organizations and how people—including themselves—are affected by them. They therefore base their actions on personal experience and instinct. In the past this was enough, or so it seemed: administrators moved up the ranks, gained experience, implicitly tested out their ideas, and, if lucky, were successful. This process may be effective if the nature of organizations and the types of decisions to be made do not change significantly over time. As we saw in the 1960s and are now seeing in the 1980s, universities are undergoing major adjustments, and successful personal experiences are not always the best indicators of future success, because the conditions of universities and thus the decisions that must be made are different from those of the past.

This became apparent in the two workshops and impressed on me the need to develop some conceptual tools, no matter how tentative, to enable adminstrators and faculty to understand the nature of leadership in universities and the role they can play in facilitating the success of the enterprise. I felt maybe this sourcebook could help in a small way by combining some analysis with examples of how administrators can and do facilitate quality teaching.

In trying to understand this relationship between the role of senior administrators and the teaching/learning process, I rather quickly moved to an organizational perspective: if senior administrators facilitate the teaching/learning process, they do it most often through their primary activities. Thus it is important to learn how their administrative decisions affect the organizational environment within which faculty teach and students learn. Given the tensions in higher education today and the anxieties and fears of faculty about their own futures, the connection between how administrators act and faculty members react has a significant impact on the teaching/learning process.

The next step was to develop some notions about the quality of life of faculty members within the university and about the styles of leadership that facilitate a desirable quality of life. I settled on four key factors that affect a faculty member's feelings about his or her relationship to the university. These factors have considerable personal impact and directly or indirectly affect classroom activities: a sense of security, a sense of ownership, a sense of pride, and a sense of intellectual vitality. For styles of leadership, I referred back to a previous chapter I wrote (Guskin, 1980) and revised it to relate leadership styles to the development of organizational environments within which faculty may or may not be creative.

A general outline of this conceptual orientation completed, I turned to searching out case studies that would reflect the topic and my orientation. I quite naturally turned to two sources—the Resource Center for Planned Change of the American Association of State Colleges and Universities (AASCU) and my own experience.

As is described in "Further Resources" by Marina Buhler-Miko, the Resource Center has been involved in one way or another with over

300 universities. The key activities of the Resource Center relate to planning for the future, developing creative teaching/learning environnents, and bringing senior academic administrators together to facilitate the sharing of experiences and the development of projects that will enable the administrators and their institutions to be more effective. As a chancellor of a state university campus and a member of AASCU, I had been chairman of the advisory committee of the Resource Center, which is composed of presidents and chancellors. I knew the work of the Center. I also knew the people involved and could assess the degree to which a particular case study was real or imagined. Through these contacts I chose three examples for development into chapters. It should be noted that these pieces are reflective of work being done in about fifty state college and university campuses throughout the nation.

I was interested in developing two chapters that would deal with academic support services and how they affect the overall university environment and the teaching/learning process directly. Here I depended more on my own experience. I chose the role of the library as the topic of one of these chapters. I was interested in showing two examples of how the library can play a vital role in the teaching process. This chapter describes the development and activities of two highly regarded teaching libraries. The second example of academic support services deals with one of the more difficult problems facing most universities — how to maintain academic standards while providing open access for students. Skill development programs have cropped up throughout the country. Probably one of the most comprehensive of these and one that has gained a great deal of national publicity is the collegiate skills program on my own campus. The development of this program fits rather nicely into the overall conception of the sourcebook.

Finally, I remembered my workshop with academic vice-presidents. They continually asked questions about how they could retain their academic values and effectively administer a university in periods of fiscal constraint. How can a chief academic officer facilitate the work of the faculty? The author of the chapter on this topic is an individual who spent sixteen years as a faculty member and administrator at Lehman College of the City University of New York, lived through the horrendous cutbacks of the 1970s as Dean of Social Sciences there, and is now a very effective chief academic officer at the University of Wisconsin–Parkside. His chapter reflects the strength of his academic values as a faculty member and administrator.

Since there were few guideposts in developing the material for this sourcebook, the product reflects my own biases. I am very comfortable defining myself as an administrator as well as an applied social psychologist. For me, there is not much difference: as a social psychologist, I was and am concerned with how educational institutions are organized, how they change, and how people are affected by them; as the chief executive officer of a university, I am concerned with these same matters. The difference is that as an administrator I act on what as a faculty member I think and write about. More often than not, my actions are consistent with my analysis; in reality, most of the time I analyze my actions after the fact in the hope of integrating this analysis into my future behavior.

Another of my biases is my deep commitment to a quality academic environment in which faculty can be good teachers and scholars, and students, good learners. I do not feel that the difficult period ahead in higher education should change our commitment to academic quality; it may mean we will have to be more careful about implementing and protecting it. I believe that if a university is not committed to quality and does not demonstrate such a commitment in its actions, it is not worthy of the name. This belief is reflected in the nature of this sourcebook.

Preparing this manuscript while a chief executive officer of a university would not have been possible without the skill and perseverance of my assistant, Joanne Sokow. She not only had the responsibility for running the chancellor's office but also had to deal with the many drafts of this manuscript. Her considerable skill in correcting my mistakes has been finely tuned over the last six years. Throughout all of this effort she has maintained her good humor and willingness to keep working with me.

Alan E. Guskin
Guest Editor

Alan E. Guskin, a social psychologist, has been chancellor of the University of Wisconsin–Parkside for the last six years. Previously, he served as provost and acting president of Clark University in Worcester, Massachusetts. He has served as chairman of the Advisory Committee of the Resource Center for Planned Change and is a member of the Board of Directors of the American Association of State Colleges and Universities.

*Administrators have considerable impact on the quality of teaching
if they are able to develop organizational environments in which
faculty members feel creative and vital.*

How Administrators
Facilitate Quality Teaching

Alan E. Guskin

The role of senior university administrators in facilitating quality
teaching is rarely discussed. Although some may feel this silence is
appropriate, my own belief is that it reflects the general scarceness of
higher education literature based on a conceptual analysis of leadership. All too often we read about how heroic individuals have carried
out the duties of office, with the benefit of hindsight; or about the
mechanics of administration, such as how to plan for survival; or about
general differences between leadership and management, with a strong
assertion of the need for more leadership.

A more helpful approach to understanding how senior university administrators can provide leadership in universities would be for
observers of higher education to adopt a more analytic approach to
leadership and illumine it with good case examples of how leaders can
and do facilitate the work of universities. Within this framework, the
role of senior administrators in facilitating quality teaching becomes a
legitimate and desirable area of discussion: first, because it enables us
to see the connection between administration and teaching; second,

because administrators do often consciously attempt to facilitate quality teaching; and third, because the effective aspects of this facilitation are most often indirect rather than direct support of individuals and their teaching interests.

To analyze and describe the role of administrators in facilitating quality teaching, we must first accept an important two-part assumption: faculty members on the whole are bright and desire to be good teachers, and the quality of their teaching is more dependent on the quality of their lives as faculty members than on the techniques of the teaching process. It follows, then, that we must understand the effects of leadership styles on the university's environment, which in great part determines the quality of life of faculty members and thus indirectly affects the quality of teaching.

Quality of Life of Faculty Members

Beyond faculty members' teaching abilities and levels of expertise, there are a number of significant factors in organizational life that have considerable impact on the quality of their teaching. I will discuss four such factors and indicate how each of these is susceptible to influence by administrators. These are:

- Feeling of security about their personal futures
- Sense of ownership in the university
- Feeling of pride in their university and colleagues
- Sense of intellectual vitality

Security. It is quite obvious to everyone connected with higher education that this decade may very well see considerable reductions in university enrollments followed by substantial budget decreases. The reaction of faculty members is obviously one of deep concern — not only will fewer faculty members be hired and granted tenure, but also tenured faculty members may be terminated for fiscal reasons. The result of this reality may be more meetings to discuss what can be done, to challenge budget allocations, to decide which positions will be cut, and so on. The psychological reaction to these events is an increased sense of insecurity among many faculty members. There are many possible effects on their teaching — faculty may spend time in class discussing the problem, they may have less time to prepare for their classes and carry out scholarly activities, and they may well redirect their creative energy from the classroom to the internal university political arena. The results of these reactions almost certainly would be a reduction in the quality of teaching and also a lessened enjoyment of teaching.

Administrators can and should play a significant role in reducing the insecurity of faculty members. Most significantly, it is the responsibility of administrators to develop fiscal controls and studies that enable a university to make the maximum effective use of its resources during a period of budgetary constraints. Providing aggressive leadership in this regard is extremely important.

Developing fiscally sound measures in isolation, however, could lead to the faculty's sense that fiscal managers are taking control. Worse yet, it disregards a very significant factor in developing the most effective utilization of resources — the collaboration between the faculty and administration in dealing with fiscal constraints. Because most of a university's fiscal resources are allocated to the instructional area, significant savings can occur only when there is cooperation between the academic area and the fiscal administrators.

Even with such cooperation, the majority of faculty members feel a sense of very limited influence in the fiscal arena of the institution. They can only support or oppose the decisions of the leadership. It is extremely important, therefore, that faculty perceive and have confidence that their university is properly managed fiscally. This feeling, in a time of financial difficulty, will not occur by magic; rather, it will be the direct result of interpersonal contact, adequate communication about problems and the measures being taken to deal with them, and, most important, consistency in the discussions about what is happening and in the implementation of university policy. Abrupt changes, major financial reductions that are rescinded under pressure, policies requiring fiscal stringency implemented without prior notice or obvious need, perceived inconsistency in application of fiscal policies or budget hearings — these actions are terribly disconcerting to faculty members and increase their sense of insecurity, which directly or indirectly affects the quality of their teaching.

Senior university administrators who understand this and act accordingly create within the university an environment where faculty can be concerned but not insecure about their future and where faculty can collaborate in activities to increase the university's financial solvency while devoting most of their energy to teaching and scholarship.

Ownership. University faculty, like almost all professional people, become integrated into their organization when they share a common set of norms and goals. Surely, faculty are concerned about salaries, fringe benefits, and working conditions, but these factors are not usually critical in determining their commitment to the university. Faculty members view themselves as performing the essential activity of the university; more often than not, they view the administrative and support staff as performing activities to help them in their work.

A governance system that emphasizes the role of the faculty member as a professional person with primary responsibility for the key elements of a university's mission—teaching and scholarly activities—will have a strong impact on the faculty's conception of their sense of ownership of the university and, in fact, on the effectiveness of the entire educational enterprise. Another way of stating this is that faculty members who have a sense of ownership in the university develop a feeling of responsibility for the manner in which they and their colleagues act and, therefore, affect the quality of teaching at the university. Such a sense of ownership is created through a shared governance system when faculty and senior administrative leadership of the university collaborate on key decision-making matters. This collaboration occurs in the elaborate faculty senate committee system and the interaction of the key administrators within that system. It is fostered by the mutual respect that results from day-to-day interaction of administrators and faculty leaders.

The direct impact of such a sense of ownership on the quality of teaching can be seen in the tenure decision-making recommendations of the appropriate faculty committees, in the merit evaluations by peers, in the collaboration of faculty and adminstrators when planning new programs, and in the faculty leadership's support for difficult administrative fiscal decisions about which they have been consulted.

- A faculty personnel committee that shares ownership in a university will take great care not to grant tenure to an individual whose teaching, scholarship, or service is below par.
- While merit dollars are often a modest part of salary increases these days, merit ratings still have considerable psychological impact. Through merit ratings, the peer review system can encourage and emphasize quality teaching as well as scholarship and service.
- The extent to which new academic programs are adequately funded determines in considerable measure the capability of the faculty to feel and be creative, to test out new teaching strategies, to risk failure, and so on. Yet new programs require the allocation of scarce fiscal and human resources. Collaboration by faculty members and administrators in the development of new programs encourages consensus on program alternatives and facilitates the sense of shared ownership.

- Fiscal policies that could create considerable turmoil within the faculty and thereby lead to faculty disenchantment and reduced likelihood of implementation can be more readily implemented if faculty leaders are consulted in a climate of shared ownership.

In short, faculty members having a sense of ownership in a university make better curricular and personnel decisions, have more pride in the university, and have a greater sense of power about their roles in the university. The key to developing this sense of ownership is a shared governance system. One of the most visible signs of such involvement occurs during the planning processes initiated within the university.

Pride. Although a sense of ownership is an important factor in developing pride in one's institution, clear indication that academic quality is important to the university is, perhaps, the key factor in developing in the faculty a sense of pride in themselves as professionals and in their university.

Such an indication of quality can take various forms:

- Individuals receiving tenure and promotion are deserving of it.
- Academic standards for students are maintained even in the face of lowered student skill levels and potentially declining enrollments.
- Programs created and presently implemented by the faculty are recognized by others outside the institution as desirable.
- Teaching quality and scholarly endeavors are held in high esteem by other faculty and the university generally.
- Public pronouncements of the university reflect an emphasis on academic quality.

Obviously, institutional pride and self-pride will be developed only when the claims of quality have substance and a striving for excellence is a reality. The assertion of these values without evidence of support for them will create cynicism, not pride.

The relationship between the sense of pride in one's university and the quality of teaching if often fairly direct. Not only is it more likely that faculty members will expect more of and give more to their students if they feel proud of the academic values of their university, but they will also be more likely to communicate a positive image of the university itself to their students. This, in turn, will make students feel more positive about the university and the quality of education they are receiving and also will increase their motivation. To close the circle, motivated students, being more stimulating to teach, will encourage better teaching. Yet another aspect of pride is that faculty members who possess it are less likely to be defensive about themselves or their students and, in all probability, will be more receptive to ways in which to become more effective teachers.

Increasing pride, however, requires more than the development of a sense of ownership and an institutional commitment to quality. It requires a faculty understanding of the reality of other universities. A problem in this area is that many universities hired a large percentage of the faculty in the 1960s, and the experience of such faculty is limited to service at one university. Combined with the lack of faculty mobility, this circumscription leads many faculty members to feel that the problems of their university are unique to their campus when, of course, most are the result of the peculiarities of universities as organizations and are held in common by many universities.

This is an interesting problem, but unlike many other difficulties these days, there are potential solutions; for instance, creating faculty exchange visits, providing resources so that younger faculty can attend conferences and conventions where they can share notes with friends and colleagues, and hiring new faculty who have had experience at other universities.

Intellectual Vitality. Intellectual vitality is probably the single most significant characteristic of a good teacher. There are many ways in which this vitality can be facilitated. The most common is the encouragement of the faculty members' scholarly and creative activities within their own disciplines. The implicit assumption in this support, usually valid, is that the creative scholar-researcher is the type of learner who makes a good teacher. This leads many university leaders to talk about the importance of developing and rewarding teacher-scholars.

The intellectual vitality of the teacher-scholar can be facilitated in a number of ways beyond the formal research project. Emphasis on seminar programs with outside lecturers is important; special lecture and cultural series featuring presentations by faculty members for their colleagues can be important; travel money to attend conferences and small grants of seed money can have significant impact, particularly in the small to medium-sized university.

Intellectual vitality can also be generated through planning, particularly in curricular areas. Nothing is more exciting to many faculty members than discussions and debates regarding the future curriculum changes that their university should undertake in order to be more responsive to both student and faculty interests. Many people wonder why faculty members spend so much time and are willing to stake so much on the implementation of one set of ideas. Faculty members are ideologues in the true sense of the term — their primary concerns are in the area of ideas and, therefore, they will vigorously contest issues that to outsiders seem insignificant or irrelevant. The intellectual vitality of faculty members, which is so essential to teaching, leads to a heightened sense of the importance of the proper role of ideas in university life.

Further, an important aspect of the intellectual vitality of a faculty member resides in the academic standards that can be maintained in a classroom and the ability of students to achieve at desired levels. Within the present educational environment in almost all universities, this means a major concern for upgrading the skills of incoming students.

Administrative Styles and Organizational Environments

While most discussions concerned with enhancing the quality of teaching have focused on teaching methods, we have taken a very different perspective: quality teaching is directly and indirectly affected by the nature of the organizational environment in which faculty members work, that is, by the quality of their professional lives. We have discussed a number of key factors in the life of faculty members and each time emphasized how administrators can enhance them. The overall conclusion that can be drawn from this discussion is that administrators facilitate the quality of teaching through the creation and maintenance of an organizational and academic environment within which faculty can achieve feelings of security, ownership, pride, and intellectual vitality.

For better or worse, at most universities the organizational environment is significantly affected by the leadership style of the senior administrators, particularly the president. Without going into great depth, I would like to present three leadership styles and discuss the type of organizational environment each might create and, in turn, how such environments might affect the quality of life of faculty members and, therefore, the quality of their teaching. It should be emphasized that these leadership styles indicate a predominant emphasis; rarely is any individual a pure type. Moreover, an individual president will likely use all three styles at different times while emphasizing one overall. These three prototypical styles are: the hero, the mediator, and the team leader (Guskin, 1980).

The Hero. The hero's style is explicit in much of the literature on universities and seems to represent a nostalgic view of the powerful presidents of yesteryear. It is also a style that is based on our youthful, uninformed images of what a leader or powerful figure is supposed to do (Sarason, 1972). People who act in this manner may not be dictatorial or authoritarian in outlook but merely feel that the president is required to make all the key decisions in a university. Except in certain limited circumstances, this leadership style is not very effective because it usually results in a lack of delegation of authority. Lack of delegation produces weak senior administrators who are not able to provide the president or others with the knowledge or human skills to make good decisions or to have their own subordinates implement the decisions that are made.

Heroes make good newspaper copy. But the heroic college president is usually placed on a pedestal. Since subordinates fear the immense potential power of the president, they may work to isolate the president and to reduce presidential influence on institutional direction. While it is possible that this heroic style was effective in more stable historical periods when goals were clear, when universities were insulated from significant external influences, and when presidents could execute their decisions unilaterally, the present situation in higher education is much too confused and fluid for such a style to be effective.

The effect of this style, all too often, is a very hierarchically oriented university—especially in the administration—and a lack of vitality throughout the institution. The latter results from a tendency for subordinate administrators not to take risks and not to respond to situations in which policy has yet to be formulated. For the faculty, this response by administrators means higher levels of uncertainty in areas affecting their lives.

Often administrators under the heroic president increase the insecurity of faculty members in financially difficult times by conveying, intentionally or not, a sense of fiscal uncertainty to faculty members who can do little if anything about it. Rather than trying to deal with their own anxieties about the future and creating a more helpful environment in which faculty can be effective teacher-scholars, administrators afraid to take risks attempt to avoid the blame by discussing ad nauseam the budgetary problems and how they negatively affect the university.

In brief, the heroic administrative style creates an organizational environment in which decisions are made by only a few people. Because of this centralization, relatively few decisions are made throughout the organization. Further, the administrators to whom faculty have access feel relatively powerless to influence policy directions, thereby making faculty representatives feel insecure about events and feel even less able to influence their organization. In this type of organizational environment, the anxiety of faculty members about their own futures—a feeling which, as we have discussed, can have significant impact on teaching—is compounded by the tendency for them not to have confidence in the administration of the university and to feel relatively powerless to change the predicaments in which they find themselves.

The Mediator. Another style of presidential leadership is that of mediator, in which the chief executive tries to resolve disputes between the diverse units through mediation. In this style, "the leader is mediator, a negotiator, a person who jockeys between power blocs trying to establish viable courses of action for the institution" (Baldridge and others, 1978, p. 45). This style, which is used by all presidents at one time or another, tends to emphasize a continuing equilibrium between the competing units, a maintenance of the status quo, rather than forging a new consensus or attempting to influence the university to move in new directions. The mediator style as the primary presidential orientation is very common in large universities where the diversity, number, and influence of units are great; where history and tradition are strong; and where the ability of the president to influence new or altered directions is extremely limited.

The organizational environment created by this style of administration tends to be marked by a movement from crisis to crisis caused by the conflict between significant campus units. Crises are resolved after clear battle lines are drawn. There is also a tendency for the success and failure of units to be determined primarily by the ability of the dean or chief administrators to be effective in the internal warfare of university politics rather than as a result of university priorities and overall university interests.

In extremely large research universities, alternatives to this organizational environment may not be readily apparent. At the same time, the force of tradition and faculty prestige may compensate for the weakness of a dean or department chair, thereby reducing the potential for neglect of a high-priority academic unit.

On the other hand, at less prestigious universities, and particularly those that are not extremely large, the mediator style reinforces the continuing conflict between units; enhances the potential for inconsistent policy directives that could result from such issue-by-issue, crisis/conflict resolution; and increases the uncertainty that faculty may feel regarding the stability and direction of their university. These liabilities would exist even if there were a strong shared governance system.

With this style of leadership, the tendency in a period of high uncertainty is for crisis and conflict to increase and for faculty members to become involved in the conflicts. When faculty are involved in crises, they feel greater insecurity and may redirect precious time and energy from teacher-scholar activities to essentially nonproductive internal conflicts.

The Team Leader. The third style is based on the president's role as a team leader of a group of decision makers. While mediation and many different forms of persuasion are often utilized, the primary emphasis is on creating an interpersonal environment among senior administrators where there is mutual respect, a strong delegation of authority, and a great deal of mutual influence among senior administrators and the chief executive. While all leadership, of whatever style, takes place in an interpersonal context, this decision-making process places major emphasis on developing the relationships between key decision makers and making the senior administrative group a vital and powerful force in the development and implementation of policy. Hence, this style is based on a team approach to decision making in which the senior administrators and president make decisions together; in which policy matters are, for the most part, initiated by senior administrators and their interaction with the president; and in which viable policy decisions emerge from the president's ability to lead the group.

In this approach, the president is more likely to be concerned with the process by which decisions are made than with specific decisions. The expectation is that, in the long run, such a decision-making environment will produce better decisions than an environment in which the president is involved in specific decisions that reflect his or her opinions on any isolated issue.

This style of leadership is developed through the tone of interaction, an agreement on overall priorities, the acceptance of mutual influence, the knowledge of how others operate, the ability of the president to relate to senior administrators individually according to their own particular styles and needs, a little charisma (but not too much), and, ultimately, a willingness by the president to make a decision if there is no other way to reach agreement among the senior administrators. Under such conditions, a president can have a great deal of influence, but so do the senior administrators who report to the president. In fact, it is because the senior administrators of the university are so powerful and because they operate as a mature, decision-making team that the president can influence and even alter the direction of the university on key issues. In other words, the president can influence the senior administrators to use the considerable power of their offices in implementing a specific policy. It should be obvious that this type of leadership is not passive but, rather, is assertive within a team approach to decision making.

Through its emphasis on strong delegation of authority to senior administrators and mutual influence between the president and immediate subordinates, this style of leadership makes a clear distinction between the use of authority and influence. The process-oriented style of the team leader emphasizes the use of influence and attempts to deemphasize the exercise of authority.

The emphasis on strong delegation of authority combined with a team approach and mutual influence leads to an administrative style that facilitates accessibility to and accountability of administrators. In theory, and, one hopes, in reality, the individuals to whom authority has been delegated (for example, the senior academic officers) are highly accessible to faculty generally and particularly to faculty leaders. In an environment where mutual influence at all levels is highly regarded, the ability of faculty representatives to have influence with key administrators is greatly enhanced. This administrative style should encourage a shared governance model, and, if marked by a concern for developing teacher-scholars, should play a key role in developing the intellectual vitality of the faculty.

However, what differentiates the approach of the team leader from the mediator is not necessarily the relationship to the faculty but, rather, the ability of highly influential senior administrators to work with each other to achieve common, university-wide objectives — to be accountable to each other and, as a group and individually, to the president. It is the striving for consensus of the senior administrative team that sharply reduces the likelihood of rancorous inter-unit conflict and that combats the crisis mentality that typifies so much of higher education today. The leadership of the president is obviously a key to this consensus, as is the ability of each administrator to participate in an environment of mutual influence. The major difference, then, between the mediator and team leader is that while both delegate authority, the mediator does not lead those to whom he delegates, that is, the mediator does not forge a team and a policy direction, while the team leader does.

Under desirable circumstances, the presidential style of the team leader creates an organizational environment that:

- increases the knowledge base on which decisions are made because those directly affected by a decision have ready access to the decision maker;
- increases the confidence that faculty (and middle-level managers) have in the operation of the university because they know they can have influence on the direction of the university if they choose;
- decreases the need for administrators to pass along high levels of uncertainty by continually emphasizing budgetary woes because faculty generally have confidence in how the university is being administered;
- increases the likelihood that faculty members will focus on their roles as teacher-scholars;
- increases the likelihood that faculty members will feel proud of their institution because of their influence within it;
- increases the likelihood that faculty members and middle-level managers will take risks by suggesting alternatives to present practices, by preparing new programs, and so forth.

While it is not always true that a well-administered university in which faculty have a sense of pride, power, and participation will be highly creative in its educational programs, creativity is more likely to flourish in such an environment than in almost any other. At the least, there is a greater potential for creativity in such an institutional environment than in one marked by insecurity, conflict, crisis, and low risk-taking.

Introduction to the Remaining Sourcebook Chapters

The importance of specifying the manner in which faculty members and senior administrators orient themselves to the university is that these perspectives directly involve the relationship between administrators and faculty and thus relate to the role of administrators in facilitating quality teaching. By increasing in faculty a sense of security, sense of pride, sense of ownership, and intellectual vitality, administrators help develop a faculty more likely to be stimulated and thus better able to teach or to be more open to improving the quality of teaching. In such an environment, faculty are not afraid to criticize their own work and seek help if they need to.

Therefore, the primary role of senior administrators in facilitating quality teaching is by enhancing the quality of the environment in which faculty members work; by supporting new programs, by stimulating faculty, staff, and students to plan for the future; and by providing adequate resources, even in times of distress, to reinforce new ideas or programs.

Since most faculty are committed to developing a quality teaching and learning experience for their students, a positive university climate that enhances the quality of their own institutional lives will facilitate these commitments. This thesis is basic to this sourcebook and is reflected in the chapters within it.

There are many areas of university life that could be included in this type of sourcebook. Each of the programs or perspectives chosen for inclusion is oriented to creating an organizational environment that facilitates good teaching. In these chapters, emphasis is placed on four perspectives that deal with the creation of such a university environment:

- the key academic administrator and how his or her work can facilitate the faculty's work
- academic and institutional planning as an essential point in time for the involvement of faculty and administrators in the development of creative organizational environments
- the development of essential academic support units that create both the necessary educational resources and the university-wide commitment to achieving quality teaching—the maintenance of academic standards that encourage quality teaching and the availability of support services that enhance effective classroom performance in students
- the development of a sense of pride in and realistic expectations about one's university through comparative experiences at other universities

These four foci were chosen to emphasize how administrators can facilitate quality teaching. In the second chapter, a chief academic officer, Lorman Ratner, is concerned with the dialogue between faculty and administrators. It is through this dialogue that a university consensus is built for the acceptance and maintenance of key academic values. In his discussion, this dialogue is extended to the necessary relationship between teaching and research and the administrator's role in curricular development and faculty recruitment. Quite appropriately, he ends with a discussion of fiscal realities and the maintenance of quality and draws upon his experiences at Lehman College of the City University of New York (CUNY) as well as his three years in Wisconsin. His conclusion is that the quality of the university environment is especially critical in a period of retrenchment. In Ratner's view, the decision at CUNY to save individual faculty jobs at all costs (as against maintaining support units, research perspectives, and so forth) may have severely hampered the ability of faculty members to teach effectively. He concludes that "to the extent that the quality of instruction influences the quality of students and to the extent that the quality of the institution affects the ability of its proponents to argue in its behalf, we must protect that quality." This statement is an important one for university administrators and faculty to remember as we enter the fiscal difficulties of the 1980s.

The relationship between faculty and administration in institution-wide planning is the focus of the third chapter, by Marina Buhler-Miko, director of the Resource Center for Planned Change. Based on her experiences as a consultant in implementing the center's Futures Creating Paradigm at many public colleges and universities, she develops the theme that such planning has the potential to create a sense of community in a university as well as to stimulte concrete plans to deal with potential futures. Miko describes the work of the Resource Center in "Further Resources."

The facilitating role of senior university administrators is almost always highlighted in major academic planning activities. In Chapter Four Thomas Hegarty and James Young present a case study of academic program planning at their college. Part of a nationwide effort of ten universities coordinated by the Resource Center for Planned Change, their case is a good example of how faculty, particularly with the arrival of a new president and vice-president, can be stimulated and challenged. It is an indication of how senior administrators and faculty, working together, can develop a creative organizational environment that can enhance the quality of teaching.

One of the key components in developing a creative academic organizational environment in a university is the clarity of the institution's commitment to appropriate academic standards for its students. By providing such, the faculty and administration facilitate a faculty member's ability to maintain his or her own integrity and pride. In Chapter Five Ben Greenebaum analyzes the issue and presents a case study of the development at the University of Wisconsin–Parkside of the Collegiate Skills Program, which requires all students to have a minimum university-level skill, and describes how this program has affected both students and faculty.

Another key element in a creative academic environment is students' ability to access resource materials, particularly in the library. Easy access facilitates a faculty member's ability to utilize such resources in the teaching process. In Chapter Six Carla Stoffle describes two well-known teaching libraries. She discusses how they developed under the leadership of library directors and supportive senior administrators and what effect they have on the teaching/learning process.

Pride in one's university is often the result of personal experiences at other campuses, experiences from which meaningful comparisons can be made. As faculty mobility decreases, so does the likelihood that faculty will have experiences at other campuses. In Chapter Seven Charles Vail presents a program of intercampus faculty exchanges based on the premise that even a few days' experience at another campus, combined with presenting one's own institution to visiting colleagues, will enhance a faculty member's knowledge of his or her own as well as another university. The comparison increases his or her sense of pride in the home institution—a simple program and idea with a powerful result.

References

Baldridge, J. V., Curtis, D. V., Ecker, G., and Riley, G. L. *Policy Making and Effective Leadership: A National Study of Academic Management.* San Francisco: Jossey-Bass, 1978.

Guskin, A. E. "Knowledge Utilization and Power in University Decision Making." In L. Braskamp and R. Brown (Eds.), *New Directions for Program Evaluation: Utilization of Evaluative Information,* no. 5. San Francisco: Jossey-Bass, 1980.

Sarason, S. B. *The Creation of Settings and the Future Societies.* San Francisco: Jossey-Bass, 1972.

Alan E. Guskin, a social psychologist, has been chancellor of the University of Wisconsin–Parkside for the last six years. Previously, he served as provost and acting president of Clark University in Worcester, Massachusetts.

*It is through a continuous emphasis on dialogue
within the administration and between
the administration and faculty that
a university-wide consensus can be
reached and maintained.*

Creating Shared Values Through Dialogue: The Role of the Chief Academic Officer

Lorman A. Ratner

It has often been stated that the 1980s are the harbingers of hard times for education — especially higher education. A decline in the traditional college-age birth pool and decreased support for higher education from public and private funding sources are merely the most generally cited evidence of a growing malaise. For those colleges and universities whose endowments are not in the hundreds of millions of dollars or whose application-to-acceptance ratio for students is below five to one, the 1980s promise to be a sobering time indeed. If declining enrollment and diminishing financial resources characterize the academic world for most of us in higher education, in the next ten to twenty years we must determine the impact of those conditions on all aspects of academic life. Maintaining quality teaching and our commitment to quality in all aspects of university life may be the most important and most difficult challenge. Striving for quality education should be viewed both as a worthy ideal and as a practical necessity.

High quality will attract students to our universities and could soften the impact of smaller pools of potential students. High quality will help those who speak for our universities to be more persuasive in their efforts to convince those who fund those universities of the importance of their investment. How a chief academic officer can help to preserve and promote quality is difficult to determine. The actions of the administrator in this sphere take him or her beyond the usual realm of activity that makes up the routine of daily administrative life. As budgetary pressures increase, administrators will have to turn more, rather than less, to dialogue with their colleagues, both administrators and faculty. The importance of such dialogue is so fundamental that many of us either overlook it or assume it; to do either, however, is to misunderstand the importance of sharing ideas. In times of expanding budgets is it easy to achieve consensus because there are enough resources for most of the needs. In fact, no substantive agreement on priorities is even necessary. Constricting resources, however, create a greater potential for conflict and therefore require more dialogue to achieve a consensus about both general directions and specific issues. It is through steady emphasis on dialogue within the administration and between the administrators and faculty that a university-wide consensus can be reached and maintained.

Establishing and then maintaining dialogue in an academic community on any particular issue is a slow process, and the conclusion reached is often difficult to predict. Dialogue reduces the opportunity to command and replaces it with the necessity to persuade. To the administrator convinced that he or she knows best and who is eager to assert leadership and achieve a quick result, using this mechanism to effect change will be frustrating. But the nature of a university, especially in times of declining resources, makes the administrator who leads by command less effective and leaves the administrator-as-persuader as the more desirable and realistic alternative. It is with this view of the role of the academic administrator and this condition of the academic community that I address the basic concern of this volume — the administrator's role in influencing the quality of instruction in the university.

What follows is my prescription for how an academic administrator can promote quality instruction and preserve and promote the quality of a university, even though financial resources may be shrinking. It is based on personal values and personal experience, and I make no claim for its wisdom or universal applicability. Rather, I offer these views as an example of an academic administrator's efforts to identify matters of importance and to promote dialogue regarding them that will lead either to their acceptance, in part or whole, or to their rejection, in part or whole.

Relationship Between Teaching and Research

While most academics accept the idea that teaching and research are interdependent and value that relationship, they disagree as to the proper balance between the two. Indeed, what I term the proper balance differs among institutions, depending, among other things, on the mission of the institution and the individual faculty member's or administrator's perception of that mission. At times the teaching-research relationship has been characterized as a conflict. According to this view, the faculties divide into those who promote and are promoted on teaching and those who promote and are promoted on research. The more administrators and faculty create mechanisms that serve to divide the two activities, the more difficult it is to establish their interdependence. Even institutions whose primary mission is teaching must recognize that good teaching requires faculty who are in some way involved in research. It is all too easy for the faculty whose only audience is the classroom to become too comfortable with their ideas and perspectives; they become too often teachers and too seldom learners. A good teacher must continually test ideas on peers as well as on students. Peer criticism is vital if natural arrogance, exhibited on occasion by most of us who teach, is not to make us overbearing. Research is important to teaching for a number of reasons, but perhaps the most important is to keep reminding the faculty that the teacher must remain always one who also learns.

In their effort to improve teaching, some universities have developed centers to assist faculty in their attempts to improve their classroom performance. Having a center concerned about the quality of teaching has considerable value. But we must be careful to avoid permitting such a center to become the vehicle for faculty who proclaim a strong interest and expertise in teaching to set themselves up in juxtaposition to faculty whose interest and strength are in research. The center's greatest contribution to quality teaching is to promote dialogue among faculty and administrators in the university on the issues related to what constitutes high-quality teaching and how it can be engendered. The academic administrator must play a key role in promoting and focusing that dialogue.

The Rewards System

Perhaps the most significant of all factors relating to the teaching-research tie is the degree to which, based on their values and attitudes, faculty and administrators emphasize that relationship in the university's rewards system for faculty. Since the rewards system in a college or university can influence the quality of teaching, the chief academic officer must work with faculty to make clear the value of the teacher-scholar. While we are used to arguments about the criteria for tenure and promotion whose premises separate teaching and research, faculty and administrators must nevertheless recognize the close bond between the two. This is not to suggest that evaluation of the classroom performace be abandoned and evaluation of only research be undertaken, but rather that teaching and research be viewed holistically. Dialogue leading to shared attitudes concerning the value of teaching and research is vital in order for faculty and administrators to ensure that the rewards system in the university is clear to all concerned. The chief academic officer must initiate or reinforce such dialogue. He or she must also be willing to make difficult personnel decisions that emphasize the concrete reality of this holistic perspective.

If the university's faculty and administrators value the teaching-research tie and make it the keystone of their rewards system, they must provide assistance to their colleagues in their efforts to meet the university's standards. The chief academic officer can, for instance, assign funds received from grant overhead to a faculty committee for the purpose of encouraging faculty research. Faculty must be able to travel to national and regional meetings to present papers and exchange ideas. Faculty in each discipline can be encouraged to establish faculty research seminars to provide an opportunity to learn from colleagues in other institutions as well as within their own. A grants officer skilled in the development of research proposals and aware of likely funding agencies can do much to assist faculty in receiving the financial support that the university may be unable to provide. Such support tangibly demonstrates that the teaching-research relationship is viewed by faculty and administrators as part of their shared values.

Curricular Development

Although keeping administrators out of direct involvement with curricular matters is a widely accepted attitude of faculty and probably many administrators, the setting of curricular goals — the evaluation of how well a curriculum is fulfilling the purposes for which the faculty created it — is an activity that a chief academic officer should seek to establish. Such an activity is properly the concern of both administrators and faculty. The general university curriculum and the specific program array of academic departments should be approached as a dynamic, evolving structure. Curriculums should always be undergoing review and periodically undergoing revision. By working with faculty on a university-wide committee on curricular review, the academic administrator can keep the goals of the curriculum before the faculty. A faculty concerned with curriculum review and committed to change where necessary will better understand the place of their courses in the university's overall effort to educate students. It should help faculty to remain aware of the ways in which what they learn and what they teach transcend the course description and contribute to a broadly conceived view of higher education. To the extent that a broad view is shared, the quality of teaching improves. That view than becomes a shared value and provides another topic for dialogue among faculty and administrators — a dialogue promoted and supported by the chief academic officer.

Faculty Mobility and Personnel Recruitment Policy

Part of the conventional wisdom in contemporary academic administrative circles is the assertion that as colleges and universities stop growing and, in many cases, become smaller, all or nearly all faculty will be tenured. Some argue that, as a result, there will be no place for the younger, perhaps more enthusiastic, teacher and the more active researcher. While most faculties will not increase and probably will decrease, I doubt that the faculty cast of characters will be as constant as is often suggested. Faculty will retire; will leave teaching for other professions, especially in fields such as business and engineering; and, perhaps more importantly, will move to other colleges and universities. Often the most mobile will be the institution's best teacher-scholars. How these faculty are replaced is a vital concern to the health of the institution and, therefore, is a concern and responsibility both of the faculty and the academic administrators.

Here again, faculty-administrative dialogue is vital in making sound university decisions. There are a number of choices available as to the level of the replacements. Faculty and administrators may opt to authorize recruitment of lecturers, thereby increasing administrative flexibility and reducing the institution's budget. Vacancies also may provide the opportunity to bring in young assistant professors, or they may be seen as a chance for the institution, at a time when positions are scarce in many fields, to upgrade the quality of its faculty by hiring established, proven teacher-scholars. Most faculty and administrators find it necessary and, perhaps, good to recruit in the first and second categories noted above, but I would suggest that if the quality of teaching is not to be lessened, they should also pay some attention to the third category, the proven teacher-scholar. Teaching and research skills, after all, are learned over time. If institutions lose their most skilled teacher-scholars and replace them exclusively with those who are just beginning to master the art, the quality of instruction will suffer.

As with the teaching-research relationship and curricular review, recruiting of new faculty is primarily a faculty concern, and any worthwhile change will result only if the faculty wish it to occur. Nevertheless, the chief academic officer has an important role to play. In this instance the role is to persuade faculty that the addition of some senior-level faculty is in their interest and in the interest of their institution. Also part of the administrator's role is to make the opportunity for such recruitment possible by managing financial resources in such a way that the funds are available for senior-level faculty to be added to the university's payroll. Determining when a department has a proper balance of senior and junior faculty is one of the chief academic officer's most difficult tasks; this decision calls for far more qualitative than quantitative judgment. To reach the wisest decision, academic officers must rely less on the rational and analytical tools of quantitative analysis and more on dialogue among faculty and academic officers.

Fiscal Realities and the Maintenance of Quality

For academic administrators, the most significant challenge of the 1980s is maintaining the quality of education in the face of decreasing financial resources. If my analysis of the relationship between teaching and research is accepted, then the academic administrator has the even more difficult job of allocating scarce resources without damaging the quality of instruction more than necessary. The temptation to separate teaching and research grows as resources shrink and as it becomes necessary to save money without reducing the *quantity* of instruction. Reduced quantity would mean a loss of student credit hours, which in turn could lead to the loss of more financial resources, and so on. We must consider that if we significantly restrict funds for faculty travel to scholarly meetings, cut back on the appearance of guest speakers on campus, increase teaching loads to the point where faculty can no longer engage in research, decrease the library's book budget, and decrease the support services available for scholarship as well as teaching, we will seriously damage the intellectual climate of the university. Damage to that climate will cause faculty to be less involved in learning and thus reduce the *quality* of instruction.

Shared values must be preserved, and those values provide the chief academic administrator with a basis for making financial decisions. Those of us who experienced the large budget reductions at the City University of New York in the 1970s faced such decisions. For obvious reasons, our first thought was to preserve jobs and avoid the loss of student credit hours. The decision to cut all budget categories before reducing staff or the quantity of instruction may have been so damaging to the intellectual climate of the institution that, in retrospect, we see that it may have been neither the wisest nor the most humane course of action. If the value of the teacher-scholar does not become the key principle to be asserted in the face of fiscal crises, then all will question whether it is indeed a value held by the faculty and administrators who make up the institution.

In any event, the chief academic officer confronted with major budget reduction faces the most difficult of decisions in attempting to serve the interests of the institution and its people. I have posed a dilemma from which there is no easy escape. If you must cut, what do you cut? I contend that we should not jump too quickly to the answer "anything and perhaps everything but personnel." As noted in the introduction to this chapter, to the extent that the quality of instruction influences the quantity of students and to the extent that the quality of the institution affects the ability of its proponents to argue on its behalf, we must protect that quality.

Conclusion

Assessing the chief academic officer's role in influencing the quality of instruction leads to discussion of that officer's role in general.

In stressing the importance of dialogue as the key characteristic of college and university life, I have meant to suggest that all faculty and administrators should promote and participate in that dialogue. A sense of separation, of distinctiveness based on role, between faculty and academic administrators is inevitable, but the gap between the two must be as narrow as possible. A good system of shared governance, respected by all parties, is vital, especially in personnel matters. A way to narrow the gap lies in a budget development process that allows faculty extensive opportunity to discuss their needs and goals and that provides for equally extensive faculty discussion of why and how budget decisions will be made. Finally, academic administrators should take the time to remain as much a part of the intellectual process as possible.

In addition to being managers, academic administrators must consider teaching their own courses, engaging in some research, participating in faculty seminars, and being involved in discussions centered on curriculum evaluation and revision. In these ways, among others, administrators participate in the dialogues that I have characterized as the essence of university life. So engaged, the academic administrator has the best chance of exercising the maximum influence in those dialogues. Persuasion is the best tool and perhaps the only real tool available to academic administrators as they seek to facilitate quality instruction as well as meet the other responsibilities of their office. In the years immediately ahead, the need for identifying shared values among faculty and administrators will be greater than ever. If we value quality in the university, we must agree on what constitutes that quality and how we can protect and enhance it.

Lorman A. Ratner, a historian, rose over a sixteen-year period through the ranks from assistant professor to professor to chairman to dean of social sciences at Lehman College of the City University of New York. Since 1977 he has been vice-chancellor and dean of faculty at the University of Wisconsin–Parkside and professor of history. He remains an active teacher and scholar.

A futures planning process that actively involves faculty fosters a sense of university community and enhances the teaching environment.

Futures Planning and the Sense of Community in Universities

Marina Buhler-Miko

It is the thesis of this sourcebook that college and university administrators can facilitate better teaching by improving the quality of life of the organizational environments within which faculty members work. The concept of a senior administrator as a leader actively involving his or her institution in endeavors that enhance the quality of the environment points us toward the question, What endeavors or what processes can and will improve an institution of higher education today? The experience of the senior administrators who have worked with the Resource Center for Planned Change of the American Association of State Colleges and Universities has been that its Futures Creating Paradigm is one of these processes. Whatever goals have emerged from each institution's efforts in futures planning, it has been clear that the planning experience itself has been in and of itself a product. All the faculty and administrators who have been involved have benefited enormously for having had the experience of planning for the future. The environment of the institution has, therefore, changed as a result of doing futures planning.

Given the need to search constantly for relevant and up-to-date institutional programs, I believe there is great value in searching for relevant, creative future goals for our colleges and universities. But it is also true that if our colleges and universities are to be viable, productive, and creative organizational entities in the future, the procedural and structural values inherent in *how* we organize ourselves in order to pursue the development of goals are equally important (Richardson, 1974). It is, therefore, the thesis of this chapter that colleges and universities must plan so that their teaching, scholarship, and service missions are viable for the future educational needs of American society and so that the very act of planning fosters a humane, creative teaching and learning environment. In this chapter I will present an analysis of how futures planning can facilitate the development of a sense of community in a university and how, in turn, this can lead to a creative teaching and learning environment. Following this, I will describe a particular planning model, the Futures Creating Paradigm, that has been successfully implemented at a number of university campuses.

A Word About Planning on Campuses Today

Planning on most college and university campuses today is most often viewed and practiced as an aspect of management. It is usually relegated to institutional research offices where administrators trained in operational research make planning into model integrated data systems, where studies are carried out setting planning objectives against student enrollment and retention data, budget projections, and faculty productivity patterns. Such studies assume that those who have set such planning objectives have carefully studied future academic program needs. Actually, as the need for a futures paradigm has shown, this seems not to be the case. Consideration is often not given to what societal trend data indicate about program needs, nor is the planning closely related to the actual teaching program. Often, it does not enter into the necessary collaborative efforts with the faculty upon whom the quality of the academic program depends.

Futures Planning and the Building of Community

Let us now look at how a planning effort can of itself be a way to improve the health and vitality of the organization as a whole. Behind

Guskin's analysis in Chapter One of how administrators can affect the quality of teaching by developing organizational environments that improve faculty sense of security, pride, ownership, and intellectual vitality, stands an assumption about the state of higher educational institutions today: Colleges and universities are troubled environments. I think he is right! The more I work with campuses from Maine to Southern California, the more I hear the strains of disillusionment with the students, a particular discipline, and/or the institution as a whole. Occasionally, there is a bright spot—a faculty member who is excited about his or her work and who has excited others. Occasionally an administrator has exerted some leadership and initiated a set of activities that has sparked creativity in faculty. But for the most part our institutions are not in very good shape. No one knows this better than the senior administrator who hears the same stories over and over again from the various corners of his or her institution. One of the main problems seems to be that faculty, staff, and students in many of our colleges and universities do not feel a sense of community within their campuses. This feeling can be traced to the lack of interest in building communities on the part of those who work in university environments today. As one faculty member of a medium-sized urban college put it to me not long ago, "No one gets involved in anything anymore around here. We are all 'burned out.'"

John H. Westerhoff and Gwen Kennedy Neville, in their book *Generation to Generation,* describe a group of people who do not seem to fit anywhere as maypole dancers. "These maypole dancers are among a growing number of persons in American culture who have been jarred by experience and their reflections out of their subcultural homes and have become estranged from their ethnic group. They find themselves like dancers around a maypole, celebrating their newly discovered freedom and their commitment to cultural change by painfully hoping that somehow a new pattern of life, meaning, and community will emerge so they can stop their frantic dancing" (1979, pp. 78–79). To a large extent the faculties of our colleges and universities are maypole dancers. Many were jarred out of their subcultures when they chose to go into academe; research has shown that few come from academic families. Many celebrated their commitment to societal change in the 1960s and now feel caught in institutions and professions that hold them economically but have lost their earlier appeal. The one characteristic all maypole dancers have in common is a feeling of isolation and separation. As Arthur Levine (1980, p. xviii) puts it, "In the extreme it [meism] robs them of their ability to see common problems and to work together for common solutions. The problems grow worse, and people feel victimized, coming to view their problems as a form of personal harassment." What is needed then is to work at building a new pattern, a new meaning, and a sense of community.

There are many definitions of community but the most inclusive seems to be Robert Nisbet's broad statement that community is "a lasting sense of relationships among individuals that are characterized by a high degree of personal intimacy, of social cohesion or moral commitment, and of continuity in time" (Nisbet, 1973, p. 1). My tendency is to add to this those aspects of community that enable a group of people to take action. For me, a community, and the sense of community, begins with the sharing of key myths that lead to a set of values about which a group of people are willing to "be intentional." It is a place where people are willing to interact and take responsibility for each other and the consequences of those interactions. It also sets up for itself some ground rules that are understood and found valuable by those involved because the rules facilitate the interaction, growth, and development of the individuals and the whole. A community also has the capability to be political in the effort to improve itself and/or deal with its problems. I do not intend the word *political* to mean simply "a clash of wills that are defending a plurality of private interests"; rather, I mean "the clash of wills in their struggle to ascertain and establish the social good and create the order of community as a whole" (Richardson, 1974, p. 112). Finally, a community has a commitment to maintain itself and what it stands for into the future. In its relationship to the larger society, a community, particularly a college or university community, has a commitment to provide the learning that can lead to needed changes.

Planning models can assist colleges and universities in the creation of a sense of community, and through this a healthy quality of life for faculty members as well as improved teaching and learning for students. Among the reasons for this are the following:

First, a good planning model asks faculty trained in various disciplines and drawn from all parts of the institution to *examine what they think*. A part of this examination is the refining of ideas on future trends in key areas — ideas that are intellectually challenging. At another level, the faculty must examine the values that they hold about teaching; learning; their college; and themselves as scholars, thinkers, and human beings.

Second, a good planning process requires faculty and administrators to *interact* about the ideas they generate. As they present their ideas about future trends, colleagues from different disciplines get the chance to debate ideas with each other, an activity that is all too rare in academe. Also, during the planning process persons from the registrar's office or from counseling offices have an opportunity to air their points of view. For example, counselors and faculty start to talk to each other about the quality, character, and goals of the students. During such interaction a common set of ideas has the potential to develop.

Third, a good planning process requires that the faculty and administrators *look at the college as a whole.* Faculty do not often have a chance to see the institution from a holistic vantage point, or hear administrators discuss the decision sequence for approving a program.

Fourth, a good planning process requires faculty and administrators *to make choices* and get involved in a complex set of decisions. For instance, they must decide which future trends are likely, which are to be encouraged, and what they mean to the institution. Then they must decide what the institution's response to these trends should be — they must plan strategy, determine feasibility, and make practical suggestions that have the optimal chance for success.

Finally, a good planning process encourages faculty and administrators alike to *take responsiblity* and develop a sense of ownership for what they have developed. This occurs, in part, because individuals know they have participated in the development of the plan. This process also facilitates the taking of responsiblity because the experience of planning itself has changed the people involved. Furthermore, the participants develop respect for the people with whom they have worked. In the end, responsiblity for the planning and its outcomes is not forced upon an individual but, rather, is something one acknowledges and takes credit for when one has been involved in work well done.

There may be still other ways in which such planning processes work to create a sense of community. Nevertheless, one must agree with Nisbet that a sense of community gives legitimacy to authority and function. Without the sense of community and the sense of ownership it creates, plans, no matter how intricate and sophisticated the planning process, will not be accepted for the future direction of a college or a university, nor will they have much impact on the effectiveness of the faculty's teaching or on the students' learning.

The Origin of the Futures Creating Paradigm

In the fall of 1975, when the Resource Center for Planned Change first started as a project funded by a grant from the W. K. Kellogg

Foundation, it took its mandate of being resourceful for planning and change to the academic vice-presidents and vice-chancellors of the approximately 340 institutions in the American Association of State Colleges and Universities (AASCU). What it heard and continues to hear from the network of these academic administrators is the following:

- Senior academic administrators need means for working out sets of policies that will assist them in making operational decisions regarding program directions, resource allocation, and personnel. Existing procedures tend to emphasize fiscal resources and personnel decisions over academic programs, although it should be the other way around.
- Senior academic administrators felt the need to understand where their college or university was headed and how they could steer it in directions that would make it responsive to the educational needs of present and future students. Administrators knew that they were being reactive, that most programmatic changes were often based not on sound educational judgments or societal trends analyses but on personalities, politics within and among academic departments, and, in some cases, on the vagaries of key state politicians. As senior administrators, they knew that if they were not looking to the future of the institution, no one else could be expected to do so.
- Senior academic administrators knew that any effort on their part to be involved in the key programs of the institution — whether instructional, service, or research — had to involve faculty.
- Senior administrators also knew from long and, in many cases, bitter experience with faculty committees that launching a major effort on a campus required a structure which was sound and easy to communicate to large groups. Planning efforts ending in ideological standoffs and no consensus on a set of goals or degenerating into turf fights between departments are not activities that administrators want to set into motion. Administrators wanted planning models that would illumine the best courses of action and yield positive results.

The basic outline of the Futures Creating Paradigm was built between 1976 and 1977 with the help of the late John Osman, consultant to the Brookings Institution, who possessed an extensive background in futures research and participatory planning for state and local governments. Through the active involvement of Osman and the Resource Center staff (Kent Alm, consultant Sipora Gruskin, and myself) at meetings of senior academic administrators and in some cases on the home campuses of the academic vice-presidents from AASCU institutions, the Futures Creating Paradigm was built. Readers who are familiar with procedures of systems research will note that many of the stages of the planning paradigm are adaptations of practices in that field. However, the underlying principle of the Futures Creating Paradigm is one of participation, that is, ways in which the technical procedures of systems research could be used by large groups of people in a manner that would build institutional consensus about the goals being constructed.

The result was a paradigm for futures planning. This paradigm is a set of generic stages based on a set of assumptions about the nature of the planning needed by institutions of higher education that seek to establish policies by which to direct their future. We strove to make these stages generic because we were (and still are) after the essential steps that an institution could take to plan for its future. These generic steps enable senior administrators at colleges and universities to undertake the difficult task of institutional planning with the confidence that the essentials had been thought through. We meant the generic steps to be a guidebook to which they and their committees could refer.

We also strove to create the generic steps and assumptions for planning so as not to interfere with — but in fact allow for — the individual purposes of each campus. In fact, this has proved to be the case. The Futures Creating Paradigm has been used for a great variety of purposes by a large number of very different colleges and universities. It has allowed each of those campuses to develop management processes and procedures appropriate to its needs. The model has been used at such campuses as Mayville State College, Mayville, North Dakota (enrollment of 750 students) in response to the Commission of Higher Education to all the colleges in that state to plan for their individual futures; it is currently being used by Governor's State University (enrollment of 4,400 students), a comprehensive urban institution outside Chicago, to provide long-range programmatic information to the resource allocation and management planning required of all higher educational institutions in Illinois; it has been used by North Carolina Central University (enrollment of 4,980 students), a predominantly black institution on the outskirts of Raleigh–Durham, to provide the self-study reporting required by the state; it is currently being used by the University of Maine at Machias (enrollment of 730 students), the only higher educational institution in Washington County, Maine (a county as large as the entire state of Connecticut), to assist them in their Title III–supported efforts to develop and expand their educational offerings to that remote area of the state. The list of institutions that have tried parts or all of the Futures Creating Paradigm is extensive. Because the paradigm has proved to be a generic planning document, it is adaptable to a variety of institutions. Where there are senior administrators concerned about the future of their institution—its programmatic viability and organizational health—futures planning has proved and is proving to be an effective tool.

Assumptions and Stages of the Futures Creating Paradigm

The Futures Creating Paradigm is based on a set of assumptions drawn from futures research, organizational development, and effective political practices. Since the writing of the original guidebook, the assumptions have undergone continuous review and change based on our experience in working with the paradigm. College and university futures planning should:

- *be based on societal trend projections and value shifts.* Colleges and universities have a basic mission to educate, but the information communicated in that educational process and even the programs themselves should change as society changes. Colleges and universities should look to these societal trends and shifts in the value system for ideas and guidance concerning areas of new program development.
- *be participatory, involving a critical mass of the colleges' key faculty and administrators.*
- *recognize the anticipatory abilities of individuals* working in groups and allow creative ideas to surface. Planning based on quantitative data may be helpful, but it should not override the conceptions that individuals have of the future shape of programs for their own institutions.
- *be structured* so that the activity has a set of stages with a clear rationale that lead to a set of results. In order to involve large numbers of people effectively, the expected set of activities must be laid out for all to examine so that people can understand what is expected of them, assume roles, and work toward ends.
- *be systemic* so that the whole institution is looked at as a whole. It is important to predict what effect plans for one aspect of the institution will have on the other parts.

The Process of Futures Planning and the Ten Stages

The process of futures planning moves from initial ideas to a set of potential objectives, to a new set of policy directions for the college or university. Planners begin by:

- gathering together the best trend and value shift data they can find
- "brainstorming" about possible ideas for new programs suggested by those trends
- formulating those ideas into possible objectives
- building scenarios and strategy sequences suggested by those objectives
- applying a series of feasibility concerns to those objectives
- deciding which objectives become policy for the college

Defining Societal Trends and Value Shifts — Stages I and II. The planning process begins with the gathering of data on societal trends and shifts in the value system that faculty consider relevant to higher education and their institution. Once the trend areas have been established — for example, faculty may decide to deal with trends in the areas of global affairs, the economy, energy, the environment — committees are established to work on analyzing alternative trends in a particular trend area. It is recommended that trends be looked at from the international, national, regional, and local points of view. Of course, one level of information may be more pertinent to one trend area than another. This is particularly true of the need for local economic data for state colleges and universities.

The extent and nature of the work done at this stage depends on the expertise of the individuals involved and the time provided. For example, an urban planner looking at regional economic trends can utilize his or her professional expertise to provide direction and substance to a working group. Similarly, sociologists and psychologists may work on defining key value shifts and give the entire intellectual community of the institution the benefit of ideas and concepts central to their disciplines. For all faculty involved in trend research, this stage may provide the opportunity to carry out research of relevance to the university and present it to their colleagues throughout the campus, something they may never have had the opportunity to do before.

Developing Policy-Making Matrices — Stages III and IV. Once the trend and value shift data have been assembled, groups of faculty and administrators begin to work on how particular trends and value shifts may affect various sectors of their college. The two-dimensional matrices shown in Figures 1 and 2 help planners make judgments about the effect of particular trends on curricular offerings, the kinds of students they will be teaching, the public service programs they may want to develop, the external resources they may have available to them, and so on. Statements of possible effects of trends are written into the cell of the matrices. Planners begin to see patterns of ideas develop, and they acquire an understanding of the effect trends will have on all the sectors of the institution. For example, the same economic trends that will lead to needed curricular changes will influence the external resource capabilities and internal allocation concerns of the college. As a natural result of this activity, planners begin to see the

Figure 1. Policy-Making Matrix — Societal Trends

Trends (Regional / National)	Curriculums	Faculty	Students	Athletics	Research and Development	Public Service	Internal Allocation	Facilities	External Resources	Administration	
Global Affairs											
Government											
Population											
Environment											
Energy											
Economy											
Science and Technology											
Human Settlements											
Work											
Lifestyle											
Women											
Participation											

Figure 2. Policy-Making Matrix — Value Shifts

Regional	Values / National	Curriculums	Faculty	Students	Athletics	Research and Development	Public Service	Internal Allocation	Facilities	External Resources	Administration
	Change										
	Equality										
	Pluralism										
	Responsibility										
	Quality										
	Inter-dependence										
	Freedom										
	Foresight										
	Localism										
	Knowledge										
	Goals										
	Leisure										

systemic nature of good planning. For example, suggested change in curriculum may affect the type of faculty expertise needed and may even suggest directions for public service programming, or vice versa. For many faculty, this process may be their first opportunity to see the complexity of the organization in which they work and the way that various changes affect the whole.

Formulating Institutional Objectives — Stage V. Stage V involves analyzing the ideas which planners wrote into the cells of the planning matrices and formulating from them a set of potential objectives for the curriculum, faculty, instruction, research development, and so forth. In other words, planners summarize the ideas in columns of the matrices put together in Stages III and IV.

Reviewing Compatibility—Stage VI. Stage VI asks planners to review the objectives developed in Stages IV and V (and the values implicit in them) and determine their compatibility with the present mission of the institution. An analysis of the proposed objectives gives planners a sense of emerging patterns in the objectives. It also enables planners to anticipate early in the planning process possible conflicts between proposed objectives and institutional mission, conflicts between proposed objectives and perceived trends, conflicts between two different proposed objectives, and other possible problem areas.

Developing Alternative Scenarios—Stage VII. Stage VII is a part of the planning process that draws on the imagination of planners. It is called scenario building, and it asks planners to write scenarios for each objective. It asks planners to use vision and imagination in conceptualizing what their institution would be like if a particular objective were realized. It allows for those in the planning group who are idealists as well as planners to work out in some detail what they hope to see happen to the institution if they are permitted to offer certain programs. There are always faculty and administrators at every institution who feel a strong sense of responsibility for the future. These are people who are often ignored in planning processes because they are not given any specific role to perform. And yet, their very passion for certain programs may light a spark in others. Stage VII of the planning process gives them and others the opportunity to expand on those ideas in a form that allows the other planners to visualize future programs and understand more fully the possibilities implied by them.

Constructing Alternative Futures—Stage VIII. Stage VIII of the planning process is the strategy stage—constructing alternative futures. It asks planners to put aside the substance of the programs they are considering and ask such questions as: What steps need to be taken before the program can be implemented? What internal or external bodies (committees, boards, legislative committees, central office approval) have to approve it? When should faculty hiring or retraining take place? At what point will the program need start-up funds and how much? In this stage, planners think through such questions, determine courses of action, and then put those concerns and activities in sequence, that is, into a series of steps to be carried out at specific points in time.

We also feel it is wise for planners to create several alternative series of steps in case an approach runs into some problems during implementation. The best way to think through these steps is to plan backwards and ask such questions as: What activity takes place last, before this program is up and running? What is the one before that? In this way, one can plan back into the present. When one must deal with many activities, decisions, and people, it is often better to start in the future and plan back toward the present. The process enables individuals to envision the planning sequences they need to develop.

An important part of Stage VIII is the production of events to create interest in and support for new programs. For example, if there is interest in creating a new program in Middle Eastern studies, planners could arrange to have a group of scholars and politicians working in this area come to campus for a week-long series of forums on Iran, Afghanistan, Saudi Arabia, and so on. The very presence of these people may generate enthusiasm and support for the program and facilitate implementation decisions, which otherwise might take months to occur.

Foresight — Stage IX. In this stage, planners are asked to think through carefully the long-term effects on their institution of a particular objective. Planners should consider what kinds of students will attend the institution if, over time, these types of programs predominate. This is a very important consideration. As the demand for career-training courses increases, there is a real question as to whether some of our institutions will cease to be colleges and universities and become something else. Responsible planners, and particularly chief academic administrators, must look at the long-term effects of such choices on their college or university.

Feasibility — Stage X. This stage of the planning process deals with the analysis of all the potential constraints and the ultimate feasibility of implementing the series of objectives. This is the final step before a decision is made to implement an objective or to discard it as not feasible. We advise planners to look at internal constraints by asking such questions as: Are there faculty to teach in this program? Will the faculty as a whole approve it? Can the financial resources be found to implement it? We recommend that an institution also look at the external constraints and ask a series of questions suggested by the direction and concerns of the larger society. Once these constraints are reviewed, then planners and policy makers can decide which objectives may become policy.

The Policy Plan

The approved objectives become the future policy directions for the institution. The plan should have the following six elements:

- Statements of institutional policy composed of agreed-upon objectives
- An understanding of the feasibility concerns attached to each objective
- A set of alternative futures or a strategy plan for each objective
- Scenarios that describe at length the effect on the institution of each implemented objective
- A statement of the compatibility of each objective with institutional goals, value shifts, and other proposed objectives
- The supporting trend and value shift data underlying the policy for the institution

By participating in the planning process, faculty and administrative teams gain a much clearer understanding of their institution. They know a great deal more about the present as well as the future status of the plan, the hidden values and purposes of each sector of the institution, the kinds of students they have, and the forces at work for and against the college in the community and at the state level.

Concluding Remarks

The planning process involved in implementing the Futures Creating Paradigm leads not only to the development of viable objectives and program plans but also assists colleges and universities in the development of a sense of community. This sense of community evolves from faculty and staff examining what they think about the future of their institution, interacting on a continuing basis about these ideas, looking at the university in a holistic manner, making choices about their future, and, finally, taking responsibility for the plans they have developed. As presented in the first section of this chapter, it is these five characteristics which generally form the basis for the development of a sense of community.

Finally, it is important to emphasize that the success of the Futures Creating Paradigm rests on the degree to which participants in the planning process view it and their professional activities as learning endeavors. For me, learning comes from a combination of openness to life and an ability to make commitments to the pursuit of understanding. It takes place outside as well as inside the classroom in the interaction of people with different values and different ideas.

If the basic value of a university as a community of learners is not accepted by faculty and staff, then no matter how much we are involved in a planning process, a sense of community will not develop and the university will be, at its very core, troubled. Therefore, it seems of the utmost importance that we reestablish this community of learners not only in the way we conduct our teaching but also in all the other forms and functions that we develop on the campus.

References

Levine, A. *When Dreams and Heroes Died: A Portrait of Today's College Student.* San Francisco: Jossey-Bass, 1980.
Nisbet, R. *The Social Philosophers: Community and Conflict in Western Thought.* New York: Crowell, 1973.
Richardson, H. W. "What Makes Society Political." In J. Moltmann, H. Richardson, J. B. Metz, W. Oelmuller, and M. D. Bryant (Eds.), *Religion and Political Society.* New York: Harper & Row, 1974.
Westerhoff, J. H., and Neville, G. K. *Generation to Generation.* (2nd ed.) New York: Pilgrim Press, 1979.

Marina Buhler-Miko is the director of the Resource Center for Planned Change of AASCU. She is one of the original staff members of the center, where she has played a major role in the development of the Futures Creating Paradigm reported in this chapter. She also directs the national Academic Program Evaluation Project (APEP) described in Chapter Four.

SUNY College at Potsdam, participating in a national project with nine other institutions, is strengthening critical student skills through sound academic planning.

Teaching, Learning, and Academic Program Planning

Thomas J. Hegarty
James H. Young

As higher education moves into the 1980s, educational institutions are in increasingly greater danger of being enveloped in, and of inadvertently perpetuating, anxiety-producing, morale-reducing, and organizationally degenerating concerns. However, the faculty and administrative staff of a university can choose instead to focus their attention squarely on contemporary concerns which must be faced even in the 1980s: on the quality of student learning, on the increasing pressure for evaluation both of teaching and of programs of study, and on the necessity for implementing curricular change even in an era of scarcity and limitations.

One way in which SUNY College at Potsdam and nine other colleges and universities are attempting to cope with these concerns is through the Academic Program Evaluation Project (APEP). The project was initiated by the Resource Center for Planned Change of the American Association of State Colleges and Universities (AASCU) and the ten institutions, with the help of a grant from the Fund for the Improvement of Postsecondary Education (FIPSE).

In this chapter we will give a brief, general review of the Academic Program Evaluation Project and then discuss in some depth how the project evolved at Potsdam. Throughout we will focus on the planning activities at Potsdam that facilitated quality teaching and on the role of faculty and administrators in enabling this to occur.

The Academic Program Evaluation Project

Basically, the development of APEP is a response to the critical questions university educators are being asked about the worth and meaning of a college degree. The answers given to this question in the past have focused most often on student acquisition of knowledge in specific academic disciplines rather than on the processes of thinking and intellectual abilities that apply to all fields. Many feel that, in our swiftly changing world, students need to master the abilities to communicate, analyze, synthesize, quantify, and value in order to grapple successfully not only with their academic disciplines but also with the expanding knowledge requirements of their future lives.

As part of its search for more effective ways to define and evaluate the baccalaureate degree, the Resource Center for Planned Change of AASCU explored these needs and questions with its network of senior academic officers representing over 300 state colleges and universities. The APEP evolved from these efforts and has outlined a number of important goals and steps to reach them.

The goals of the project are to enable each college and university to: specify the generalizable outcomes of their baccalaureate degrees; enable the faculty in all disciplines to explore together, make explicit, and develop effective means for teaching, learning, and utilization of those mature skills hitherto departmentalized and taken for granted in different specialties; look at how well they are teaching such skills as communicating, analyzing, synthesizing, quantifying, and valuing; and plan for changes in education important to the long-term career success of their graduates.

To implement these goals the project has developed a five-stage process or paradigm:

Stage I: Developing conceptual definitions of key thinking skills common to all subject matter, using the available substantive expertise as well as classroom teaching experience.

Stage II: Identifying performances that indicate students' use of key thinking skills — communicating, analyzing, synthesizing, quantifying, and valuing. Further, the process provides a framework for faculty and administrators to answer key questions for major policy decision making.

Stage III: Designing and implementing means for assessing students' thinking skills and the programs where these skills are acquired.

Stage IV: Evaluating the results of the assessment of student performance and programs, comparing the results with an institution's quality standards and making judgments based on discrepancies between assessment and standards about the need for programmatic change.

Stage V: Developing a policy at each institution to ensure student acquisition of key thinking skills.

Among those applying, ten state colleges and universities, diverse in size and geographic location, were chosen to participate in the Academic Program Evaluation Project. The participating institutions are: SUNY College at Potsdam (New York), North Adams State College (Massachusetts), Ramapo College (New Jersey), Western Carolina University (North Carolina), Ball State University (Indiana), Southern Illinois University–Edwardsville, Western Kentucky University, Wayne State College (Nebraska), University of Nebraska–Omaha, and California State University–Chico. Each campus has a project director, most of them academic vice-presidents, and a campus coordinator, who works closely with a multidisciplinary committee of respected faculty. Their task is to adapt the general ideas, goals, and processes of APEP to the particular purposes, needs, and circumstances of their own institutions. The role of the coordinating staff in the Resource Center for Planned Change is to frame a common process, or paradigm, that will provide both consistency and flexibility for each institution's approach to defining and evaluating traditional thinking skills.

Planning at Potsdam

Planning at SUNY College at Potsdam has many roots. One that is especially germane to this topic developed from a 1976 system-wide mandate from the State University of New York to review or write new individual campus mission statements. At Potsdam work on the project attracted relatively wide campus involvement. The resulting document, completed in the spring of 1978, was, however, long and cumbersome. Although it did provide a broad view of campus direction, it did not prove to be a guide to action. In the summer of 1978, a new president and a new vice-president for academic affairs arrived and responded to college-wide suggestions that the mission statement be refined into a work of readable length that would be a road map for the institution's future over the ensuing three to five years. A large coordinating team, representative of every group on campus and various community groups and co-chaired by the vice-president and chairman of the faculty assembly, undertook the work and produced a serviceable document. The resulting mission action plan made a clear commitment to assessing student outcomes. In particular, it specified as desired student outcomes the skills of communication, analysis, synthesis, quantification, and valuing. In addition, the mission action plan reaffirmed the college's commitment to general education and a well-developed major field of concentration. Also prominently mentioned was a promise to "initiate," "modify consistent with student needs," and "continue the debate over the proper content of" a general education program.

At another level, the vice-president and the deans of the three schools of the college had encouraged discussions in departments, school curriculum committees, and an institution-wide academic affairs committee. Topics for discussion included the meaning and content of liberal arts education, general education, the roles and the scope of a major, and the relationship of liberal learning to the world of work. As a result of the various deliberations, some modest changes had already resulted in the college's general education plan.

At the same time, the college's governance system and administrative structures were revitalized through a consultative system and a team-oriented administrative structure. As many avenues for reconsideration and renewal opened, nearly everyone on campus was involved in, or significantly affected by, some effort. Opportunities to achieve long bottled-up plans seemed to be at hand. The time was right for participation in an exciting project that could focus on enhancement of the academic program.

APEP Begins

While this emphasis on self-renewal had been springing up independently at Potsdam, the Resource Center for Planned Change at

AASCU had decided that skills development within the baccalaureate program was in need of study and attention. The Resource Center had begun meeting with state university and college academic officers to develop an approach to the problem. Among those most involved in the early stages of the project were the vice-president for academic affairs and the associate vice-president from Potsdam College.

Out of a series of meetings, the Resource Center developed a draft paradigm and a proposal for a sizeable grant from FIPSE to permit ten AASCU institutions to pursue the assessment of undergraduate skills through the Academic Program Evaluation Project (APEP). The proposal was successful, and APEP got under way in September 1979, with the selection of ten institutions.

Why did Potsdam choose to apply to the Resource Center for participation in APEP? Like each of the twenty-five institutions that applied to participate, Potsdam College intended to discover how successfully its bachelor's degree programs provide graduates with academic skills. Potsdam wanted to provide information, first of all to our own community and its members who felt the need to document the impact of undergraduate education, but also to rebut the external questioners who raise doubts as to the efficacy of liberal arts education in an age of specialization. In the state of New York, educational institutions are, in general, being called to stricter accountability. The State University of New York has expressed interest in assessing learning outcomes. The Middle States Association of Schools and Colleges had already notified institutions of its region that outcomes assessment would be an expected part of self-study prior to a reaccreditation visit. In New York, the state education department, the state legislature, and legislative staff made it clear that, as they assessed the impact of dollars spent on colleges and universities, demonstrated outcomes of education were a major interest.

In addition to studying and documenting change in students' skill levels, however, Potsdam College also expected the project to permit program changes. Through an analysis of the program of courses followed by students who would be tested, APEP could lead to improvement both in educational content and in evaluation procedures currently in use. The college has taken as one of the most useful purposes served by the project the fact that the information would be available to identify areas of curricular strength and weakness. We were not interested in looking at the impact of individual courses taught by an individual faculty member; rather, we wished to see the impact on skills of typical program groupings in the undergraduate educational plan.

APEP at Potsdam

A committee on intellectual skills was formed to implement the APEP project at Potsdam. Its members included and still include representatives from the faculty assembly's committee on academic affairs, the curriculum committee of the three schools of the institution, alumni, students, and virtually all teaching specialties. The senior administrators of the college serve on the committee as advisers and resource people. Big enough to represent every interest and to make available all shades of campus opinion, the committee nonetheless proved small enough in its operation to carry out the task. Weekly sessions began in mid November of 1979. There were sessions lasting a full day or a full weekend and a few meetings on and off campus with representatives of other APEP institutions from North Adams State College in Massachusetts and Ramapo College in New Jersey. Individual members produced their own conceptual definitions, and the committee worked to boil these down "word by agonizing word," as one member described the process. The committee found that the process of discussion and compression was useful because the differences arising from various discipline perspectives were ironed out at committee meetings.

The committee began by cataloguing activities or actions that seemed to relate to one of the skills selected for discussion. Many pages of thoughts and observations were filled. The process of cataloguing served as the basis for group interaction and produced a general statement about basic process and, at last, yielded a definition of the skill.

The committee benefitted from the theories and taxonomies suggested by the staff of the Resource Center. These papers and readings provided external support for locally produced definitions when they finally emerged one by one from the group. Reading a common treatment from the Resource Center helped to provide shared vocabulary and images that advanced the building of definitions.

The order of topics with which the committee dealt merits some mention. The group began with the communication skill but deferred action on it to talk about the skills of analysis and synthesis. After much wrangling, everyone agreed that analysis and synthesis really were a single skill with two names, coexisting as "two sides to the same coin." As the committee was about to deal with the quantification skill, a committee resource person, dean and philosopher, made a splendid presentation on valuing. Quantification was, in turn, deferred while the group dealt enthusiastically with valuing in a state-supported institution. Not only was valuing seen as germane and part of our existing education but as the umbrella skill under which the other skills fit. At that juncture, the committee resumed work on communication, refined analysis and synthesis, which went through several significant changes, and then finished its first stage of the APEP assignment. The committee carried away from this early stage the recognition that the skills are closely interrelated and cannot be lightly or easily separated from each other.

Throughout the discussions, minutes were recorded and circulated widely to both members and nonmembers. These notes, which were both entertaining and useful, served to prepare the campus as a whole for the work of the committee and to keep people interested in the group's progress. One of the happy results that the campus community detected was the fact that the conceptual definitions truly reflected the distinctiveness of Potsdam. Our curriculum, which has a heavy emphasis on music, the arts, computer literacy, and library skills, was painstakingly reflected in the definitions that resulted.

After the committee had written the definitions of the five generic skills (that is, definitions built up from specific activities and actions indicative of the skill), they reversed their direction in order to establish behavioral aspects for each of these skills. The second stage of the APEP process involves deriving subcomponents of the skills so that the levels and measures of these skills can be more easily discussed and ultimately developed. As the committee moved through the spring and summer of 1980, the conceptual definitions they had first formed continued to hold up. As this account is being written, in October 1980, the committee is now in a late stage of determining locally acceptable levels of performance for the generic skills. Their recommendation on the key matter of levels requires more discussion.

The committee discovered that between the definition for the cognitive and behavioral components of a skill there is a gap; for some, a "leap of faith." There are inner, cognitive operations or mental processes performed in the five skill areas. There are also external behavioral operations that can be observed about them. The committee wrestled to describe the latter. Having developed behavioral definitions for the skills, we are now prepared to ask students, selected according to a carefully devised testing plan, to perform the operations so that their thinking can be evaluated. The students' thinking will, in theory, be tracked to the point where their skills can be partially isolated and inferred from measurable activities. Hence, our committee has gone through a process that at first produced statements about skills and is now producing specific, multiple statements about behaviors from which each skill can be observed, evaluated, and thus better taught. Acting by consensus, they have assembled operational definitions that are totally relevant to our curriculum, and which serve as an appropriate starting point for measuring how our students have benefited from it.

Role of the Faculty at Potsdam College. Faculty experience has proved to be the heart of the APEP process at Potsdam. Our faculty committee drew not only on their knowledge of what a specific skill meant in their discipline; they drew also on their position as teachers and mentors of students. This position gave them the opportunity to delve into generic skill areas each time they lectured, led a discussion or seminar, graded papers, carried on research, or prepared and participated in a public service project.

The experimental attitude of many of our faculty proved important in the light of the scarcity of research and investigation into the area of skills. Although the Resource Center found for us excellent empirical and philosophical research work on cognitive and perceptual development and even some interesting theoretical structures, nothing was found about the relationships of the five skill areas to the attainment of the bachelor's degree. Moreover, the crucial role of our faculty reinforced our commitment to institution-specific objectives. It dissipated some concern expressed by a few members of the Potsdam community at the start of our involvement with APEP, concern about the implications of participation in a national project. Faculty soon fully realized that we ourselves are planning for our future through APEP, and that we alone determine what APEP achieves at Potsdam.

The work of the committee and its interaction with colleagues in every department also dissolved the reluctance felt by some members of the community about measurement, especially the measurement of the skill outcomes of learning. Two influential chairmen had feared that measuring in general could lead to the trivialization of education, and that skill measurement might suggest a downgrading of the importance of content. In the liberal arts context, broad content as well as depth in at least one area is a tenet of faith. The committee's actions showed clearly to their colleagues that the vitality of content was not diminished; in addition to content, we were also simply considering broad-based definitions of skills that were not content-specific. The faculty now concurs with the importance of this task.

The work of the committee on intellectual skills, which is technically an administrative committee appointed by the president, has fit especially well with the work of the governance organs on campus and with the work of academic departments. The reasons for this are several. First of all, the committee has representatives from virtually every group on campus. Therefore, the committee has, in most units, a natural spokesman who is able to serve as a communication link among his colleagues. The committee sensed a great deal of interest whenever members made presentations to groups of faculty on the conceptual definitions of the five generic skill areas. At those sessions, a great number of half-buried and even well-hidden issues emerged: people spoke openly of fears regarding evaluation, of reservations about the abilities of some of their students, even of doubts about their own teaching. The discussions were and continue to be frank and helpful. APEP has enabled us to dispel some unfortunate notions few people were willing to face directly prior to our involvement in the project. As one member of the group stated it: "We found it an absolute delight to sit down not to talk about minor problems but actually about intellectual matters with all kinds of ramifications for the departments." It should be noted that such conversations were always germane to skills assessments and the outcomes of undergraduate education since virtually all of the faculty at Potsdam College are involved not only in fielding a major but in participating in general education.

Role of the Administration. As necessary to the success of APEP on the campus as the role of the faculty was the facilitating role of administrators at many levels. The president enthusiastically appointed the broad-based committee on intellectual skills and gave it complete freedom. He attended, as invited, the key meetings of the committee, proudly publicized their achievements in talks on and off campus, and created a climate in which administrators affected by APEP or by skills assessment felt free to participate in the development of detailed goals and objectives statements.

Contributing also to the success of APEP at Potsdam was the appointment as coordinator and chairman of the committee on intellectual skills an individual who had excellent counseling and listening abilities. He created the optimal conditions for free and yet purposeful discussion at meetings. The vice-president for academic affairs took responsibility for maintaining communications between Potsdam and the Resource Center in Washington, D.C. and was technically director of the project. He, together with the academic and student affairs deans, was intellectually active and visible, although not intrusive or directive at the committee meetings. The willingness of the administrators to let faculty decide contributed greatly to the week-to-week progress of the group.

Where Are We Now? In the late spring of 1980 the committee moved, in accordance with the revised APEP guidelines, into Stage III, which required a determination as to which students would be assessed for skills and also which curricular or instructional features of the program would be portrayed in order to account for student outcomes.

Over the summer a subcommittee carried out a mandate from the parent committee on intellectual skills to (1) develop an evaluation design and (2) decide on the creation or identification of testing materials that could be used to assess the outcomes of student learning in the five skill areas and would facilitate the portrayal of student programs and their analysis. A visit to the college from an Educational Testing Service consultant reinforced the already expressed preference for "home-grown" tests of student skill performances. The consultant introduced the group to the challenges of test-item construction and selection and test validity, reliability, and discrimination. When it became apparent that the committee, in the period of the grant, would find it difficult to assemble a total testing program on its own, the group decided that it was preferable to modify a commercially prepared package in such a way as to test for the uniqueness of the Potsdam curriculums.

From the time of the consultant's visit until this writing (late October 1980), the total committee has resumed its activities and is refining the skill and subskill statements to make sure that we as a college will be looking at what is important to Potsdam in the skills development of our students. The committee is working to increase general faculty awareness and involvement in modifying the testing package for Potsdam. The group and other interested colleagues are identifying appropriate generic skill areas in current methods of evaluation in Potsdam College classrooms—for example, multiple-choice and open-ended tests; essays; media presentations; artistic works or collections; performances in dance, drama, or music; as well as term papers and research papers. All seem to be potential unobtrusive means for measuring skills. In this way, any class, any student, and any faculty member can contribute to the self-evaluation process. The faculty and administration are concerned with discovering how groups of courses and programs contribute to generic skill development. Our institution is preparing for November testing, which should further help everyone at

Potsdam to see and understand the range of student performance. The results will also, of course, lead directly to an evaluation of our stated objectives and the ways in which we are striving to achieve them.

What Has APEP Done for Our College?

The Academic Program Evaluation Project has already become, for Potsdam, an important medium for creative self-evaluation. It has stimulated us to intellectual dialogue and constructive action. It has served us as a responsible guide. APEP reaffirms the fact that undergraduate education is more than distribution requirements and content and more than the acquisition of facts and formulas, important as each of these is. It is the mastery of essential intellectual skills that are transferrable from one content area to another and from the context of college to the context of life.

Our purposes also reflect our desire to be accountable to taxpayers, to our students, to their parents, and to others with concerns over how students are served. We also, however, sincerely desire to know for ourselves how Potsdam College's liberal arts curriculum strengthens or adds to the life skill of students in the five areas that we have chosen to examine.

There are other significant benefits to the college from the activities connected with APEP. Postdam College is becoming increasingly aware of the need to focus on intellectual and academic expectations. We have gained a variety of perspectives on the intellectual skills we expect our students to develop. In addition, we are sharing in the development of appropriate methodologies and strategies to help students succeed. We are refocusing our efforts on the need for our students to become independent thinkers, creative problem solvers, and lifelong learners. Moreover, as faculty, staff, students, and administrators, we are focusing on constructive goals held in common rather than on divisive political or fiscal issues.

The ultimate benefits of APEP, those to our students, are yet to be fully realized. We expect that improvements in learning for students will continuously evolve from our deepening commitment to the APEP process. As we grow in our understanding that all of us serve as facilitators of learning, and as we fully support one another to that end, we shall grow in our ability to assist students in achieving expectations that we ourselves have defined in a culturally rich and psychologically supportive atmosphere.

*Thomas J. Hegarty is academic vice-president and provost
at SUNY College at Potsdam and has been a very active
contributor to the national APEP project and to the
development of the Resource Center for Planned
Change of AASCU.*

*James H. Young is the president of SUNY College at Potsdam
and is a member of the Advisory Committee of the
Resource Center for Planned Change.*

Students who demonstrate college-level skills not only are better learners but also promote better teaching.

Improving Student Quality Through Upgrading Student Skill Levels

Ben Greenebaum

With the exception of the few institutions that are major centers for research and postgraduate training, most universities view teaching undergraduates as their chief function. Even the research universities still count teaching as one of their chief roles. The quality of faculty members and their attitude and skill in teaching are obviously important to the quality of undergraduate education. But the quality of students themselves is also a very important factor in their own education. It is student quality and a program for its improvement that are the subject of this chapter.

Good students make good teaching easier and more likely to happen. It is almost a cliché to point out that the learning process is an active one: professors may teach, but it is the students who must do the work of learning. They help each other learn as well, both in class and out, through the time-honored processes of working together to thrash out troublesome problems arising from course work and of using their new knowledge to sort out, if not settle, the rest of the world's problems. When professors see their teaching leading to visible signs of learning; when students produce solid ideas, sound term papers, or good senior theses; when graduates go on to succeed at first-rate graduate and professional schools; then the faculty members' feelings of personal success mingle with some overall pride in their institution. The process is self-reinforcing, too. Faculty members who are proud of their students and their institution will set higher standards of performance for the students and will expect more from themselves as well. Therefore, one method the administrator can use to encourage good teaching is to ensure that the students at the institution are "good."

Who are the "good" students? I will presume that most faculty members would agree that they are students who are open to new ideas and subject matter, are able to comprehend the material presented to them with reasonable speed and ease, are able to synthesize what they know without much help, and are willing to do the work required to carry out all of the above processes. There is one more characteristic that many faculty members would put into the definition of good students, a characteristic that would not have been thought about ten years ago: the good students will have a mastery of the basic intellectual tools that allow easy access to the new ideas being presented and make doing the work necessary for full mastery a task of reasonable dimensions.

Obviously, one way to increase the number of good students at an institution is only to admit students who meet rather rigid criteria. Some colleges and universities have sufficient prestige to be this selective in their admissions, but even they have complaints about the preparation of their freshman students. Many institutions, by the nature of their assigned mission, their location, or their institutional philosophy, admit a much wider variety of students and need to convert them into good students after admission.

In recent years all universities have faced the need to offer compensatory instruction. Usually the need is presented as a way of providing access to underprepared students while trying to preserve the academic quality that is absolutely necessary for postsecondary institutions. The discrepancy between the preparation that American universities have required or hoped for in their students and the preparation students have been able to get from their community public schools has varied over the years. Some students have benefited from superb high school or preparatory academy educations and enter college already having mastered much or all of the content of freshman courses. Sometimes such achievements are recognized through advanced class placement or awards of college credit; sometimes the student just has an easier transition to college and finds courses less challenging during the freshman year. Other students enter with marked weaknesses in one or more areas of their preparation.

Differences in the ability of school systems to provide advanced course work have been one cause for this variation in the ability of students; presumably these have depended upon the size of the district, the number of its college-bound students, its wealth, and the overall educational goals of its inhabitants. Other causes include nationwide changes in who goes to college, the decline in the influence of the printed word, and changes in university degree and admission requirements in the 1960s.

Collegiate institutions in the U.S. have historically had to face a gap between their expectations and the preparation of many of their prospective students. In an effort to provide access to their degree programs and to preserve the standards they set for themselves, many institutions founded in the nineteenth century included precollegiate "institutes," "academies," or "preparatory departments." For example, the University of Wisconsin had a preparatory department from shortly after its founding in 1848 until 1879 (Curti and Carstensen, 1949). At first, students as young as ten years of age could enroll, if they at least knew basic geography, English grammar, and arithmetic (through fractions). The stated intention was to turn precollegiate preparation over to the local secondary schools as soon as they were broadly established across the state.

Throughout its history, the University of Wisconsin precollegiate department was the subject of discussions of its place in the university that sound familiar to modern ears. It was clearly acknowledged to duplicate the secondary schools' curriculums, but there were large numbers of students who could benefit from the university who had no access to an adequate secondary school. The state university was felt to have an obligation to offer a route for these students to gain access to higher education. By 1879 the high school system had spread, a system of accreditation by the university had been established (graduates of these schools could enter the university without taking entrance examinations), and pressures to abolish the preparatory department were successful. Precollegiate courses in Greek and Latin remained, however, since many potential matriculants at the university still needed help in these subjects. Misgivings about the way underprepared students could meet the university's standards remained in some quarters (Curti and Carstensen, 1949). Most colleges' precollegiate instruction experienced the same fate at the end of the nineteenth century. The predominantly black colleges in the South were exceptions; they continued throughout the twentieth century to admit large numbers of students with poor primary and secondary preparation and to offer them whatever level of instruction they needed to succeed in college-level work.

As in the nineteenth century, new groups of students are now entering U.S. universities. Some of these nontraditional students are very well prepared. But some are from ethnic or cultural backgrounds that have experienced educational discrimination; some have gone through schools that are poor for other reasons; some have not taken the proper college preparatory high school courses; and some have been away from education for a period of time and have lost much of what they once had learned. To be sure, the universities are not concerned now with the students' Latin and Greek—even in 1880, the University of Wisconsin had stopped requiring these for entrance to the School of Arts. But, as it was then, the concern now is over the students' degree of mastery of what we today consider the basic intellectual tools that an undergraduate needs to succeed in college-level work.

An Approach to Upgrading Student Skills

Within the last few years there has been a good deal of discussion about the "basic skills problem" in universities, and I do not propose to summarize it here. Instead, I will use a single example of one university's approach to improving the basic skills of its students, the Collegiate Skills Program at the University of Wisconsin–Parkside, as a point of departure for our discussion. My purpose in this presentation is not to discuss the specifics of the example, but rather to look at the way academic administrators can influence the teaching process in the institution by adopting and implementing such a program. I will also look at the influence that an increase in the overall skill level of a student body can have on the quality of teaching at an institution.

The philosophy and structure of the University of Wisconsin–Parkside Collegiate Skills Program have already been described (Guskin and Greenebaum, 1979), so I will present here only those details that are essential to this discussion. As a publicly financed, commuter institution, the university offers a college education to many types of students, including many whose previous educational experiences were not of the sort that produce good students. Many other students are resuming their education after a long interruption. A significant number of this last group had been good students once, but time and disuse have pushed their knowledge and academic skills into corners of their memories. The Collegiate Skills Program is a way of giving all these students a chance, while preserving the integrity of the university's degree.

The program's rationale starts with the assumption that students who are admitted to the university are capable of succeeding at the level expected of a student earning a bachelor's degree. That statement is almost a tautology; it says that admissible students have the potential to graduate. But it also says that students ought not be judged admissible and then put into a situation in which they are sure to fail. In such a case the fault is that of the institution, not the students. The program recognizes that the verbal, quantitative, and investigative skills develop along a continuum, ranging from the skills of a toddler through those expected of a postdoctoral student or a professor. Excessive emphasis on the high school senior–college freshman level has caused many university people to forget to think about what happens after the freshman year. However, the Parkside program tries to pay attention to building skills throughout a student's career. The program does not attach a value judgment or try to assess why a student entering college may be underprepared, since the causes are many and looking for them in individual cases is counterproductive. Instead, the program tries to remedy substandard skills in entrants while simultaneously working with the schools to reduce the number of underprepared students in the future.

The purpose of the Collegiate Skills Program is to ensure that all students have the skills they need to perform at the level required in upperclass courses by the time they become juniors. The program does this by identifying five competencies — in reading, writing, basic mathematics, library research, and writing a research paper — that the faculty considered essential for students in all majors; basically, the program establishes a floor for all students. Students are encouraged to demonstrate these competencies as soon as possible; but since they are not required to do so until the time they finish their sophomore year, access for underprepared students is assured. Those not fulfilling the requirement are put on probation (after forty-five credits) or dropped (after sixty credits) in the same way as someone with a low grade-point average. Students are assisted in meeting the requirement; they are given a mandatory placement test in English and mathematics as they enter and are advised, on the basis of the results, of the appropriate sequence of courses and/or self-study to bring their skills to the level that will satisfy the requirements. A sufficient variety of instructional opportunities in courses and a learning lab are offered to allow students to bring up their skill levels to the required point in the shortest possible time.

At this writing (fall 1980) the program has just completed its third year. Students are entering, being placed, taking courses and competence tests, and occasionally going on probation or being dropped. Drop actions are appealed, sometimes successfully, or students leave and either do or do not return. An evaluation of the tests and of the effects of the freshman-sophomore part of the program is under way.

The junior-senior part of the program, which was seen as a continuation of the requirements for increasing verbal, quantitative, and investigative skills that vary with the needs of each major, is still in its earliest stages of development. Some instructors are asking for more writing; some disciplines have tightened their quantitative or investigative requirements for majors. The regular cycle of internal program reviews of all undergraduate majors is being expanded to determine skills required in upper-division courses. Library skills exercises are entering the research methods courses, and more essay exams are appearing. The university-wide attention to these upper-division skills is intended to build upon the sophomore-level requirements. Without the upperclass demands, the competence requirements may become one-time peaks of knowledge, quickly forgotten. With the development of the upperclass program, there will be a coherent university-wide system supporting the goal of capable, high-quality students completing demanding upperclass courses to become capable, high-quality graduates.

The University of Wisconsin–Parkside Collegiate Skills Program is a far-reaching one; it affects most parts of the academic and support areas of the university. Its establishment was the result of a long, collaborative effort involving faculty and administration. It is appropriate now to look at that process, again with the purpose of presenting an example from which one might generalize, rather than advocating a specific model. We will then return to examining the effects of the program on the entire institution.

Planning the Program

The role of the academic administration in the process of establishing the Collegiate Skills Program was twofold: First, the administration, working with the faculty governance apparatus, created a situation in which a sweeping curricular change could be developed and accepted by the faculty. Second, again working very closely with the faculty governance apparatus, the administration encouraged the development and implementation of the idea through allocation of administrative liaison staff and reallocation of personnel, assistance, and resources to carry out the program. At the present time, the administration's role is one of helping and encouraging the faculty to finish the development of the program while keeping the already operating portions working smoothly. The academic content of the program was and is the faculty's, a necessary condition in any quality institution of higher education; as any administrator knows, an academic program can be killed by either the faculty or the administration, but can be developed only by both.

The adoption of this particular program began with an institution-wide examination of educational directions and methods that was part of the first year of the administration of a new chancellor, a unique time for any institution. Other institutions have begun similar studies in response to changes in other administrative offices, preparation for accreditation, changes in funding situations, or just the accumulation of internal feelings that something ought to be done. One widely known example of the last is the three-year study leading to a revision of Harvard University's program of general education. In all of these situations, an administrator recognized the faculty's receptivity to program changes and initiated a collaborative planning process. The general outlines of the change may or may not be evident in the administrator's mind, but its precise nature is left to the faculty-administrative planning groups, which are given power to review the situation and recommend solutions. If the administrator believes a particular approach is appropriate, that proposal must be gently made within the planning process; in most situations low-key persuasion is the best way to influence the groups. The more sweeping a change, the more prepared the administrator must be for the recommendation to be generated by the committee as a whole. At best, compromise is the order of the day. Sometimes just such compromise is not possible and no viable program emerges.

In the case of the Collegiate Skills Program, the planning process was very broad (Guskin and Greenebaum, 1979). The faculty-student working group on academic programs isolated the basic skills problem from many faculty comments and selected the competence-based format without much prior attention to this issue from the administration. However, this issue and solution were immediately seen as consistent with the administrators' chief general concerns: strengthening academic excellence, broadening the general understanding of overall institutional goals within the university, and strengthening the way academic programs and structures supported these goals.

The process of taking the program from the suggestion stage to the status of a fully implemented program involved some of the most thoughtful university-wide discussions of the process of education that the campus had seen. First, the planning group and then the full faculty had to consider how the program would affect the education of students, the climate in which the faculty and students would work for the next decade, and enrollment. The faculty readily concluded that the program would produce highly desirable results in quality education and institutional climate and, to their credit, concluded that its effects on enrollment would be, at worst, tolerable and, at best, favorable.

Regarding enrollments, faculty members and administrators agreed that the proposed program might enable many students with marginal skills to receive a good university education and that students who could not achieve the desired competence levels by the end of the sophomore year did not belong in the university and probably would leave anyway. The student representatives embraced the proposal wholeheartedly and helped strengthen the resolve of the institution. They predicted that the program would enhance the institution's reputation for quality and thus add luster to their degrees, encourage good high school students to enroll as freshmen, and reduce the number of students who transfer elsewhere.

After the program had been adopted as university policy, a faculty-student-administration committee worked out the details of a full program. It was important for the faculty governance apparatus to choose for this committee its best-suited members, individuals who supported the program and understood the issues it involved, who were articulate, who were willing to work cooperatively, and who were respected by the faculty at large. The leaders of faculty governance and the administration discussed the appointments and had little trouble agreeing on them. The administrative and student representatives were chosen with similar care.

The implementation group's first task was to reach a consensus that the entire faculty would accept on what skills were essential for all students. Working with the rest of the university and with the local high schools, library staff and the English and mathematics faculties had to set conceptual goals and to agree on common course outlines and texts, common and cross-graded competence examinations, and cooperative ways of sharing the workloads among themselves and with the academic skills staff. In the process, not only did the mathematics and English faculties have to consider the needs of all other disciplines, but each of these two key faculty groups also had to decide among themselves the best way to impose external standards on their lower-level courses. Given the task and the broad consensus that supported it, these groups of faculty members accepted self-generated regulation of the way they conducted their sections, regulation that would have raised great protests of the violation of academic freedom if suggested by anyone outside the discipline, whether administrator or faculty member.

Throughout this part of the implementation process the active role of the administration was that of facilitator—providing staff and modest amounts of budgetary assistance, setting up a meeting, occasionally putting a word into the committee deliberations, doing a rewrite when asked. In addition, the administration was also working hard to prepare the procedural aspects of the program, making sure that record keeping, registration, and other details were taken care of by the time the students needed them. Of course, these details had to await the finalization of the committees' academic policy decisions and their debate, refinement, and approval by the full faculty.

As the program has evolved, the implementation committee has become a monitoring body. The administrative role is now to help maintain resources, ease the operational side when details need attention, and remind the group of past faculty resolutions and intentions. The administration also works quietly to keep the resources devoted to this program in balance with the resources needed for the rest of the academic program. Initially funded primarily from resources already allocated to remedial English and mathematics and from a special reallocation of fiscal resources that result from a large-scale reorganization of the administration, the skills program cannot cut too deeply into other academic areas without becoming suspect. On the other hand, once it proves its worth, it can stand up with the others in fighting for allocations during budget hearings.

The Impact of the Collegiate Skills Program

As mentioned earlier, a formal evaluation of the first two years of the competence testing program is now under way. While the results of various parts of this evaluation will not be ready for six to twelve months, there is a considerable body of nonstatistical evidence that indicates that the program is working well. This evidence enables us to begin to understand the impact of the Collegiate Skills Program on the quality of education at the University of Wisconsin–Parkside. One part of this analysis will be a discussion of how the program has improved the quality of the students. The remainder will examine other program outcomes that have strengthened the institution and particularly its teaching mission.

As noted earlier, the main purpose of the Collegiate Skills Program is to give the instructors in junior- and senior-level courses the assurance that their students can perform at appropriate levels in five skill areas. The evidence shows that the university has been enforcing its standards and that the faculty and students have been noticing the change. At the end of the 1980 spring semester, 74 students were placed on one-semester drop for deficiency in collegiate skills; these students had grade point averages that otherwise would have kept them in good academic standing. Over 400 additional students have been placed on probation; this means that they have to complete the requirement within their next fifteen credits. One must add that not all 74 ended up on drop status, since a few students appealed and were granted extensions, some finished their requirements over the summer and were readmitted, and some may have never intended to continue in the university. Few could transfer, however, since transcripts would clearly show a drop status. The number of students finding themselves on drop or probation status may decline in the future as students realize the stringency of the policy. In appealing for a waiver, more than one student stated disbelief that lack of an approved term paper would cause a drop; these students are now believers.

Even those students being dropped have accepted the program; no appeals challenged it in principle. Although a formal attitude survey of students and faculty is still in the data-collection stage, there is a good deal of anecdotal evidence that students and faculty continue to believe it will increase the rigor of their courses. The university's chancellor tells of a student newspaper editor who, initially seeking information for a story that would have been unfavorable to the program, ended up writing a very supportive article. Present student government officers, echoing the hope of the student members of the committee that established the program, have stated their belief that the skills program assures students and the public that Parkside graduates have met a standard of quality not enforced in many universities.

From the start, it was believed that the program's design had several important features that worked to the benefit of nontraditional students, who form almost half of the student body. Two important segments of this population are minority group members and older adults who are returning to education after a period of pursuing other activities. Because the Collegiate Skills Program is competence-based, it emphasizes the individual's needs and achievements. There is individual placement and advising at admission, and the requirement is that the individual demonstrate a specified level of performance. Furthermore, the program is fully integrated into the university and is required of all students. Therefore, unlike many other skills programs, this one does not single out a high-risk group, which often includes a disproportionate number of minority students, for special testing and course work. High-risk students are screened for skill problems and offered appropriate help as a part of the normal routine; therefore, there is less stigma attached to this process.

The individualized, integrated approach helps the returning adult student, as well. Many of these students, even those with good secondary school backgrounds, are unsure of their ability to reenter education and to do well. With sensitive advising and specialized support groups when needed, the skills program eases entry into the university by offering the student a challenge that is structured for early success, just what these students require to build the confidence to earn a degree.

Effects on Teaching

And what of the faculty members' perceptions of the program? Most comments and other indications seem to show that faculty members continue to expect their students to be more capable than in the past and intend to ask them to exercise their skills at appropriate levels. Part of this expectation is undoubtedly nostalgia for students with the SAT scores of the 1950s, but a great deal of it is looking ahead to the 1980s and helping its students, traditional and nontraditional, to achieve substantially higher curricular goals. Faculty members seem clearly ready to put in still more teaching effort if they see that their present push for higher skill levels produces students with better preparation for their courses.

In addition to increasing the quality of their teaching by improving the quality of their students, the implementation of the skills program has had several other favorable effects on faculty members and their teaching. In the first place, this sweeping reform of a part of the curriculum, like any such university-wide discussion of educational policy, had led to reexamination of related parts of the educational process. One is tempted to say that a "Hawthorne effect" is in force here: almost any attention to the educational process will produce better education than no attention will.

Another product of the Collegiate Skills Program has been to create in some members of the faculty a serious professional interest in skills education. As part of the implementation process, faculty members in all parts of the university have studied tests and testing, curriculums, and teaching methods. A number of papers and articles have resulted, some written by faculty members who until recently did not have much to share with their profession, but whose professional creativity and leadership ability were stimulated by the program's challenge. Their colleagues have recognized and welcomed this increase in professional creativity. As Ratner argues in another chapter of this book, the teacher who is also an active scholar in some aspect of the discipline, including the teaching of it, contributes to the teaching mission as well as to the overall quality of the institution.

There is an additional effect of the implementation and success of the program that cannot be underrated: its reception by the community, the University of Wisconsin system, and the national education community and the influence of that recognition on the faculty and students. When the program was being planned, it was well received by the local public schools; their reaction helped strengthen the university's resolve to make it succeed. When the plans were ready, the public announcement received widespread notice in the state and national media. The program was properly perceived as a bold, risk-taking step on the part of a relatively traditional though young institution to begin to solve a problem that was troubling all of higher education. Such national notice was an immediate source of pride and support for the judgment to adopt the program. It also increased the willingness of faculty to take risks in other areas of the curriculum, for example, a precollegiate minority program, substantial outreach efforts, and new academic program development.

The program was the first major attack on deficient collegiate skills in Wisconsin, and when the University of Wisconsin system established a Basic Skills Task Force in 1977, a Parkside representative was named to share our experience and philosophy. Subsequent programs throughout the state and the task force report (Lenehan and others, 1979) reflected the Parkside analysis and approach to the problem; such acceptance by an institution's peers indicates to the university's faculty and students a recognition of its quality by the rest of the state. The university's leadership has been acknowledged, both verbally and with limited amounts of funding, by the University of Wisconsin system; such recognition is quickly appreciated by all parts of any university. The system is now placing high priority on efforts to improve basic skills, both within the system and by working in cooperation with the primary and secondary schools. There is general confidence that the university's leadership will continue to be recognized.

Pride in one's university and one's work leads to greater efforts in all aspects of a faculty member's work. In turn, these efforts produce results of higher quality, which lead to increased pride; and the cycle continues. This theme has run throughout the chapters of this book. Our example, the Collegiate Skills Program, has acted both directly and indirectly, through the improvement of the overall atmosphere of the university, to improve the quality of teaching and learning.

References

Curti, M., and Carstensen, V. *The University of Wisconsin, 1848–1925.* Vol. I. Madison: University of Wisconsin Press, 1949.

Guskin, A., and Greenebaum, B. "Quality and Equality: Basic Skill Requirements at the University Level." *Educational Record,* 1979, *60,* 312–318.

Lenehan, W. L., Chambers, D. L., Clasen, R. E., Greenebaum, B., Harder, S., Kolka, J. W., Myrbo, C. L., Rice, R., Last, E., and McGahan, S. L. *Final Report of the University of Wisconsin System Basic Skills Task Force.* Madison: University of Wisconsin System, 1979.

Ben Greenebaum is associate dean of faculty and coordinator of graduate studies at University of Wisconsin–Parkside. He is a professor of physics and remains an active teacher and researcher in physics. As a faculty member in 1975–76, he was instrumental in initiating the Collegiate Skills Program.

By increasing students' library skills and collaborating with faculty
on student assignments, librarians at two universities
play an important role in facilitating
quality teaching.

The Library's Role in Facilitating Quality Teaching

Carla J. Stoffle

The primary responsiblity of college and university administrators is to
maximize the utilization of the human and material resources of the
institution in support of the educational goals of the faculty and students. As a senior administrator responsible for all academic support
and student services units, I am responsible for fostering among the
nonteaching staff a concern for and understanding of the teach-
ing/learning process and for creating an environment where the staff
are encouraged to relate their services and resources to faculty needs.
In my experience, staff and faculty in such an environment come to
view themselves as partners in the teaching/learning process. This
partnership results in the increased effectiveness of the total educational program of the university.

The library is an academic support unit that, under appropriate
administrative leadership, has great potential for enhancing the teach-
ing/learning process. In almost every college or university, the library
is acknowledged by faculty, students, and administrators as the "heart
of the campus." Yet on many college campuses the potential of the

library goes unrealized. The library becomes an underutilized, expensive storehouse. Librarians are seen as, or what is worse, perform as, keepers of the books, or, in the words of a Cambridge University faculty member, "warehouse managers" (Cubbin, 1980). Consequently, library materials purchased to support the curriculum lie unused on the shelves. Student who frequent the library often use it as a study hall or as a convenient location for a social gathering. In addition, when students have a course assignment or research paper that requires the use of library materials, they often perform poorly and spend more time than necessary. The reason for such poor performance is that most students do not have the necessary skills to effectively identify and use appropriate library materials. Compounding the lack of student skills is the lack of informed library involvement in course and assignment planning. This failure to cooperate means that library staff are less effective than they could be in helping students and providing guidance to appropriate materials. The ultimate result is that indepenent study assignments planned to enrich student learning become an ordeal with little educational benefit, much student frustration, and a great deal of extra work and dissatisfaction for faculty members.

However, on some college and university campuses around the country, the library and librarians have been able to maximize the substantial investment in library resources and services by actively working in conjunction with faculty members to improve the educational experiences of students. These libraries have adopted a philosophy of library service called the teaching library. The teaching library is one "which is not only a support service for academic programs, but which is itself actively and directly involved in implementing the mission of higher education: teaching, research, and community service" (Guskin, Stoffle, and Boisse, 1979).

Generally, a teaching library is characterized by a significant number of the following:

- A commitment to instructing students, faculty, and staff in the effective identification and use of information resources
- A commitment to bringing all library resources to bear on the development of college students into lifelong learners
- A commitment to providing access to and encouraging the appropriate use of its resources by residents in the surrounding communities
- A commitment to developing a climate of learning in surrounding communities by working with other community

educational institutions to facilitate the fullest possible use of the information resources available

- A commitment to maintaining a collection adequate to meet basic campus needs
- A commitment to resource sharing so that the campus community has easy access to materials not available in the library (Guskin, Stoffle, and Boisse, 1979, p. 283).

The core component of the teaching library is a bibliographic instruction program — the systematic instruction of students in effective use of the library's resources. The development of a successful instruction program brings librarians into frequent interaction with faculty as they work together to improve the skills and performance of students. Often, this collaboration of faculty and librarians takes the form of lectures by librarians to classes with library-related assignments. Sometimes this collaboration is extended to the active participation of the librarian in developing appropriate course assignments to aid the faculty member in attaining the instructional objectives of the course.

Two examples of institutions that have successfully implemented the teaching library concept are Earlham College and the University of Wisconsin–Parkside. In these institutions, there is a faculty-librarian collaboration that has led to educational programs of higher quality and increased faculty and student effectiveness. These institutions have been selected to illustrate the potential of libraries because they have been recognized both nationally and internationally as models for academic libraries and because they illustrate that a teaching library can be implemented in diverse environments (Tucker, 1980).

Earlham College

Earlham College, established in 1859, is a small (1,200 students) four-year liberal arts college affiliated with the Society of Friends. It is primarily a residential college, with a selective admissions policy, and a very informal relationship among students, faculty, and staff. The faculty of approximately 100 is relatively stable and is diversified in rank and age.

The library facilities at Earlham consist of Lilly Library (the main library) and the Ernest A. Wildman Science Library. Together, these libraries have about 275,000 volumes, with some 1,300 current periodical subscriptions. The staff of the library consists of 5.5 professional librarians, 3.5 clerical staff, and a large number of students.

The evolution of the Earlham College Library into a teaching library began in 1962 when Evan Farber was appointed the library director. Farber's commitment to the teaching library grew out of his early experiences, which indicated that despite the "very good teaching [at Earlham], there were many students who did not know how to find information" (Farber, 1974, p. 148). The inability of students to find information, in turn, resulted in their performing poorly on library-related course assignments and reduced the teaching effectiveness of the faculty. In addition, this lack of skills meant the existing materials and facilities were underutilized, and that fact made it difficult to justify additional budget support for materials both he and the faculty considered essential.

To correct the poor library research skills of students and to increase the impact of educational dollars spent on the library's collection, Farber and his staff began approaching with offers of assistance faculty who gave library research assignments in their courses. This assistance included everything from preparing bibliographies to having librarians teach several class sessions on how to find and use library materials necessary for course assignments. Eventually, this assistance even extended to having library staff work with some faculty on the development of their courses and the creation of assignments to reinforce the course objectives.

In addition, Farber and his staff began a concerted campaign to participate as fully as possible in other phases of the teaching/learning process at the College. This participation centered on actively reaching out to faculty — providing faculty with information about the collection, about the availability of new materials in their research or teaching areas of interest, and about the performance of their students in the library on assignments. The staff at Earlham also developed mechanisms for finding out about faculty research interests and new courses; they established collection development procedures that have brought librarians and faculty into regular discussions about what should be added to the collection. These procedures clearly define collection development as a joint responsibility and ensure that available collection dollars are maximized by knowledgeable purchasing. Other activities engaged in by the library staff in support of the faculty and the educational mission of the college include special campus events or exhibits in the library that are timed to coincide with course presentations; the sponsorship of lectures, poetry readings, and the like by faculty or off-campus personalities; displays on topics of current interest nationally or locally; and special programs to stimulate student interest in reading.

Of course, the key program of the Earlham College library is the bibliographic instruction program. The overwhelming faculty acceptance of the value of the program is evidenced by the inclusion of "competence in the skills of information retrieval and the use of the library for research purposes" as one of the thirteen educational aims enumerated in the 1973 faculty revision of the educational goals of the curriculum (Farber, 1974, p. 147). Library instruction at Earlham is now integrated throughout the curriculum and is cumulative in nature. The program begins with the testing of students' library research skills during freshman orientation week, extends to involvement in the entry-level required humanities and biology courses, and builds to providing specialized instruction in upper division courses with discipline-specific research needs. The program is noted for its course-related nature and its flexibility. No bibliographic instruction is provided for courses without library research assignments, although certainly other kinds of library support are available. For courses with such assignments, the librarians work with the faculty member to determine the nature of the instruction, the skills of the students, and the amount of time available. Then instruction is tailored to the exact needs of the individual courses. Most of the bibliographic instruction at Earlham is accomplished through lectures varying in length from ten minutes to several class sessions. In the sciences, a guided exercise has been developed that requires students to use specialized science reference works and journals to complete a number of assignments (for a further description of the Earlham College program, see Kennedy, 1970; Kirk, 1971).

University of Wisconsin–Parkside

In contrast to Earlham College, the University of Wisconsin–Parkside is a medium-sized (5,400 students) urban commuter institution in the University of Wisconsin System. The campus is only twelve years old and has an open admissions policy. The undergraduate curriculum is composed of programs in the liberal arts and sciences as well as professional programs in business, labor and industrial relations, education, engineering technology, and allied health areas. The graduate curriculum centers on master's programs in business and public administration. The approximately 200 faculty members at Parkside are relatively young; about 85 percent of them have Ph.D. degrees, many from the country's most prestigious research universities.

The Library/Learning Center is located at the center of the campus. The collection consists of over 300,000 volumes and 1,800 current periodical subscriptions. Faculty and students, through the Wisconsin Interlibrary Loan System, also have access to the library collections of the University of Wisconsin–Madison. The library staff, also relatively young, is composed of 9.3 professional librarians, 10.5 clericals, and a large number of student workers.

From the inception of the library, the staff have been service-oriented, and they engaged on a random basis in a number of activities designed to integrate the library into the mainstream of campus life. The organization of the library's activities into the configuration now called the teaching library evolved over a four-year period beginning in 1973 with the hiring of a new library director, Joseph Boisse. Boisse recognized the educational potential of the library's active involvement in the teaching/learning process and supported the teaching and outreach activities the public service staff had begun before his arrival. He encouraged the staff to develop goals and objectives for the library's service activities, and he used these objectives as the basis for budget allocation.

Like the Earlham program, the development of the Parkside bibliographic instruction program began small. Librarians contacted faculty already utilizing library-related course assignments and offered assistance. Building on a base of receptive faculty, the staff developed their own expertise and gained a reputation for being competent partners in the classroom. As student performance on library assignments improved, other faculty on campus began to seek out librarians to be involved in their courses. Now the library's bibliographic instruction program is systematic, comprehensive, and acknowledged by many faculty as an essential part of the instructional program. The program is organized into four levels with goals and objectives (competencies) specified for each level (*Bibliographic Instruction Program*, 1976, 1978). Competencies at level one are very general and concentrate on enabling the student to identify and locate the general services and facilities of the library. The comptencies of the second level are for all students a required part of the University's Collegiate Skills Program. The goal of this requirement is to ensure that all students have the ability to identify and use the basic resources of an academic library. The third-level goals and objectives are organized by discipline and are now being met in history, political science, sociology, business management, geography, communications, and psychology. The goal of this level is to provide students with the ability to identify and use the major reference tools, research strategies, and research techniques appropriate to their major fields of study. The fourth level of the program is devoted entirely to course-related needs, that is, providing instruction in how to utilize specialized library materials in order to complete a specific course assignment. Librarians offer instruction at this level in almost every discipline in the university.

The instructional methods utilized by the librarians vary according to the level of the program and the needs of the individualized course. Level-one needs are met through printed guides and a library exercise required in one of the beginning English courses. The level-two skills are taught through a self-paced basic library skills manual, which has been incorporated into a regularly offered English course—team-taught by faculty in English and library staff—called "The Library Research Paper." The level-three skills are primarily taught using self-paced manuals devoted to describing the basic reference works and research strategies and techniques of a specific discipline (Stoffle and others, 1979). These manuals are utilized generally as part of required research courses offered by faculty in each discipline. In most of these courses, librarians team-teach the bibliographic research section with the course instructor. For courses with library research assignments, the librarian and faculty member determine the types and amount of instruction needed and then tailor a lecture to meet their needs.

In addition to the instruction activities of the librarians at Parkside, considerable staff time has been spent in activities designed to support the faculty in other ways. To develop a knowledge of faculty needs and to fully integrate the faculty into the development of the library collection, the library staff have created the librarian liaison and faculty profile programs. The liaison program involves assigning a librarian to work with the library-related needs of each discipline. The librarian regularly interviews faculty members (the faculty profile) about their current research interests and course development plans. In addition, faculty are contacted throughout each semester about new additions to the collection or possible purchases in their area (Stoffle and Pryor, 1977).

Effects on Teaching

At Earlham College and the University of Wisconsin–Parkside there have been many educational benefits for faculty members and students from the integration of the library into the teaching/learning process. This integration has given students the confidence and ability to write better papers and perform more competently on all library-related research assignments. Student development of library research skills has also reinforced a lifelong learning orientation, that is, a disposition to utilize information-gathering skills to answer questions and solve problems outside the formal educational environment.

The educational integration of the library has also led to more effective faculty members. As student skills have improved, faculty have been able to make more demanding assignments and have been able to concentrate their efforts on the substantive content of their courses. Necessary library materials to support and supplement course work have been more readily available in the library. Course planning, both for new courses and for updating the content of regularly offered courses, has been made more efficient, and the development of appropriate assignments has been facilitated. Also, reliable outside feedback on student reactions and on students who are having problems with the course materials has been provided by the librarians who have worked with the faculty on the preparation of the course. Faculty reactions to the programs at Earlham and Parkside are illustrated by the following:

I have also found the [library's sociology] workbook has had an effect on the quality of independent study projects. Before, independent study students who did not have a workbook to work with had a difficult time in doing an independent study, or organizing their resources, of collecting data, and of doing a piece of sociological research. And now I find, and it's a pleasant surprise, that people who have had the workbook can organize their research, go through consistent steps, and reach point A through C in a short time and sound very intelligent and articulate in doing it.

Recently, a number of graduates who are working in the community have returned to campus to consult me or other sociology professors. They all seem to start out the same way. "Well, I've looked here and I did this and this and this and I still can't find the information I need. Should I consult X?" It's such a good thing they know what the sources are, and they know how to locate them [Gruber, 1978, p. 99].

My enthusiasm for library instruction continues to be reinforced as I work with students who are confident in their

ability to use the library extremely well, a skill that is para-
mount in the process of self-education, a process that will continue long after our students leave our campus [Harvey, 1976,
p. 32].

A working familiarity with the use of the library can
serve to achieve one of the most basic purposes of a liberal arts
college. It can truly liberate the student to be a self-starter. Bibliographic instruction, when it is accomplished in the context of
a substantive academic program and is done with practical rather
than with more formal ends in mind, really frees the student by
awakening her or him to the possibilities of the scholarly task.
The feeling of achievement when one comes across a gem of
information obtained only because one knew where to look is in
a very real sense its own reward [Farber, 1978, p. 73].

In the case of the University of Wisconsin–Parkside, an additional benefit of the library's involvement in the teaching process, according to one senior faculty member, is that the library's organization of its
instructional program and its specification of instructional objectives
became the model for the organization and objectives of the University's
Collegiate Skills Program. That same faculty member also made the
following observations regarding the role of the library:

Advanced instruction of the sort practiced here can bring
alternative models [of instruction] into the classrooms of faculty
in a variety of disciplines. Because it is almost inevitably a collaborative enterprise, it can involve faculty members in new
modes [of instruction]; it thus offers some of the advantages of
team teaching at much less expense. . . . It should be noted
that library instruction, freer by nature from the course and
credit syndrome that affects most faculty, is an area particularly
open to alternative [instruction methods]. . . . Library instruction can serve as a "carrier" for mediated instruction, computer
assisted instruction, unit mastery systems, and other instructional forms. . . . When you have a full discipline working together with a librarian, people can be acquiring new teaching
ideas and techniques without even knowing they are improving
their teaching [Canary, 1978, pp. 40–41].

Role of Administrators

Obviously, the success of the teaching libraries at Earlham College and the University of Wisconsin–Parkside would not have been possible without high-quality, active librarians and cooperative faculty concerned with teaching. However, similar programs with similar librarians and faculty at other institutions have not succeeded. One of the important reasons for the success of these programs is that they have enjoyed administrative support and encouragement from the chief executive on down through the director of the library. Both Evan Farber and Joseph Boisse were firmly committed to the integration of the library into the educational programs of their institutions and facilitated these developments through their leadership and actions (Boisse, 1978). They established, in conjunction with the staff and senior administrators, the goals of the library and then set internal priorities and redirected the library's budget. They advocated this view of the library to the faculty and other institutional administrators. Within the library they hired and rewarded staff who had teaching skills and who were committed to and involved in activities that would integrate the library into the educational mainstream of the institution.

The supportive actions and attitudes of other university administrators have been critical to the success of these libraries. Senior administrators were involved in and approved of the shift of goals and priorities for the library. The library administration was directly supported in their work, both symbolically and fiscally. Senior administrators provided moral support for the library's activities in highlighting the library when hiring and orienting new faculty, in speeches dealing with the state of the institution, and in meetings with educators and others visiting the campus. Also, the library's budget was protected insofar as any unit's budget could be during the financial difficulties of the last several years. If budget dollars became available unexpectedly, the library was high on the list for receiving a share because dollars spent in the library are expected to have a greater impact campus-wide than dollars spent in any other unit.

Of great importance to these efforts of the library staff has been the fact that both campuses foster an environment that encourages risk-taking and creativity. Faculty are encouraged to be good teachers, and they receive administrative support for teaching improvement.

In fostering the concept that the library could and should be actively engaged in the teaching/learning process, what the university administrations did not do, an omission as important to success as all that was done, was to legislate the involvement of the library or point out to faculty that their teaching effectiveness could be improved and that the library was the source of help. The relationship between the library and the educational program was left at the level of individual faculty members and librarians. Administrators trusted that if the goals and priorities of the library, the skills of the staff, and the environment were appropriate, the library would be integrated into courses where it was suitable. Patience, trust, and moral support were the primary virtues that both administrations displayed. This patient, trusting approach is critical; in the classroom the faculty are autonomous and have a considerable amount of ego and pride tied up in their teaching. The suggestion that their teaching had to be improved could have been seen as threatening.

Several points should be reemphasized in conclusion. First, the library is a powerful symbol in the academic world and has great potential for fostering educational quality if its staff members are actively involved in the teaching/learning process. Second, the academic library is an administrative unit, responsive to leadership from senior-level administrators. Therefore, as senior administrators begin to look for ways to improve the quality of teaching and learning, they should not overlook this critical campus resource.

References

Bibliographic Instruction Program. Kenosha: Library/Learning Center, University of Wisconsin–Parkside, 1976. (ED 126 937)

Bibliographic Instruction Program. Kenosha: Library/Learning Center, University of Wisconsin–Parkside, 1978. (ED 169 890)

Boisse, J. A. "Library Instruction and the Administration." In C. A. Kirkendall (Ed.), *Putting Library Instruction in Its Place: In the Library and in the Library School.* Ann Arbor, Mich.: Pierian Press, 1978.

Canary, R. "Library Instruction as a Model for Educational Innovation." Paper presented at Leadership Conference on Bibliographic Instruction, University of Wisconsin–Parkside, June 22–24, 1978.

Cubbin, G. "Fresh Priorities in Library User Education." In P. Fox (Ed.), *Library User Education: Are New Approaches Needed?* Proceedings of a Conference. The British Library Research and Development Reports, Report No. 5503, March 1980.

Farber, E. I. "Library Instruction Throughout the Curriculum: Earlham College Program." In J. Lubans (Ed.), *Educating the Library User.* New York: Bowker, 1974.

Farber, E. I. "Librarian-Faculty Communication Techniques." In C. Oberman-Soroka (Ed.), *On Approaches to Bibliographic Instruction: Proceedings of Southeastern Conference.* Charleston, S.C.: College of Charleston, 1978.

Gruber, J. *Panel Discussion.* Proceedings of the Leadership Conference on Bibliographic Instruction, University of Wisconsin–Parkside, June 22–24, 1978.

Guskin, A. E., Stoffle, C. J., and Boisse, J. A. "The Academic Library as a Teaching Library: A Role for the 1980s." *Library Trends,* 1979, *28* (2), 281–296.

Harvey, W. H. "A Biology Professor Looks at Library Instruction." In H. B. Rader (Ed.), *Faculty Involvement in Library Instruction.* Ann Arbor, Mich.: Pierian Press, 1976.

Kennedy, J. R., Jr. "Integrated Library Instruction." *Library Journal,* 1970, *95,* 1450–1453.

Kirk, T. J. "A Comparison of Two Methods of Library Instruction for Students in Introductory Biology." *College and Research Libraries,* 1971, *32* (6), 465–474.

Stoffle, C. J., Karter, S., and Pernacciaro, S. J. *Materials and Methods for Political Science Research.* New York: Libraryworks, 1979.

Stoffle, C. J., and Pryor, J. "Parkside Teaches Library Use from Orientation to Competency Requirements." *Wisconsin Library Bulletin,* 1977, *73,* 159–160.

Tucker, J. M. "User Education in Academic Libraries: A Century in Retrospect." *Library Trends,* 1980, *29* (1), 9–27.

Carla J. Stoffle, assistant chancellor for educational services at the University of Wisconsin–Parkside, is a well-known librarian who has played a significant role nationally in stimulating the resurgence of the teaching library. Prior to becoming assistant chancellor, she was associate director of the University of Wisconsin–Parkside's Library/Learning Center and head of its public service unit.

*Tri-university faculty exchanges affect the way faculty members
view themselves and their institutions and can foster in faculty
a sense of pride in their work.*

The Revolving Faculty Exchange Program: Increasing Knowledge and Self-Esteem

Charles B. Vail

Faculty attitudes are important among those influences that set the spirit
and tone of a college or university; and to the extent that attitudes gov-
ern the quality of teaching, the outlook for education in the final dec-
ades of the twentieth century may be grim. Stresses due to unfavorable
economic and demographic factors are reflected in important aspects of
faculty members' lives. Growth in institutional size and impersonality
combined with a declining sense of the college as a community bring
about uneasiness in teachers about their own work and roles as well as
those of their administrative colleagues. Faculty benefits and privileges
that would tend to mitigate the stresses are themselves in decline.

Among the undeclared privileges of past eras sacrificed to new
economic conditions is the relative ease of changing jobs and institutions in quest of accelerated advancement or better scholarly condi-

tions. The opportunity to work in more than one institution had those benefits, to be sure, but there were also special dividends beyond rank and station. Changing institutional affiliation had the salutary effect of exposing the professor to a variety of educational settings. Regrettably, a tight job market virtually eliminates easy mobility. The result has been a strong tendency to academic myopia, which, although not evil, tends to limit the professor to his or her academic discipline and own university. Under present circumstances, the faculty member tends to perceive the problems of his or her own institution as unique because there is too little contact or familiarity with any other university. In time, the perceptual restraints grow stronger, and the sense of narrowed perspectives may create anxiety. The effects upon the performance of the professor as teacher are surely negative.

The Revolving Faculty Exchange Program was instituted to compensate for this diminished mobility of faculty. Beyond the goal of providing useful experiences on other campuses, the program has sought to expand significantly the scope of learning that might be expected otherwise in traditional faculty roles. The plan is one of immersion of faculty members in the life of their own and two other universities through short but productive encounters. Time spent on other campuses lends perspective to issues observed on the home campus and establishes a new frame of reference for understanding and comparing those issues. Simple and inexpensive, the program gives many dividends, the most important of which are improved teaching and enhanced morale.

The faculty exchange program is more appropriately seen as a series of short visits rather than as some form of trading. Teams of faculty members are brought together at each of three institutions for combined inquiries. On these occasions faculty may enjoy a feeling of comradeship as they discover the differences and commonalities among their respective institutions. Away from home in another academic environment, faculty get the chance to awaken to a sense of reality about the nature of a university (including their own), to the universal aspects of the role of the teacher-scholar, and to the ultimate responsibility of the teacher to the student.

The design of the faculty exchange program was initially based on the characteristics of site visits associated with accreditation work. In such work, the declared purpose of visiting another institution is to perform an evaluation of and render assistance to the host institution. Significantly, the visitors often gain more than they deliver — or so they say—because they learn much not only about the visited institution but also, through introspection, about their own. Problems and processes are, indeed, not unique to any one institution, but are found in all colleges and universities. Also, there are fine ideas at work in other institutions that ought to be tried at home. It does not matter whether these perceptions were wholly accurate or the ideas adaptable; the important consequence is a liberation from the narrow perspectives of the home institution.

Another fixture of the academic world which influenced the faculty exchange program was the magic of consultation. Consultants grow in ability with the passage of time, and that is as it should be, but it cannot be said that they grow wiser. Good consultants expand their portfolio of solutions with each mission because they garner ideas from each place they visit. As peddlers of ideas, they harvest new ones even as they deliver from the store of old ones. The handicap of consultants is that they may have no means of monitoring the results of their past efforts, since they have no further contact with the parties involved and thus do not benefit from the value of feedback.

If, as alleged, members of visiting teams in accreditation work derive unplanned benefits, and if it is true that consultants grow in skill because of their contacts with many institutions, it would seem only logical to design visits specifically for the visitors—visits free of the self-study and case study documents supplied by the host and formal reports prepared by the visitors. Thus was born the Revolving Faculty Exchange Program.

The original network comprised Shippensburg State College (Pennsylvania), Western Kentucky University, and Winthrop College (South Carolina). These three state institutions planned and conducted the pilot program during a two-year cycle extending from 1977 to 1979. Each institution developed its own selection criteria to choose a team of six faculty members for the first year and, as the importance of including a librarian was discerned, seven for the second. No attention was given to matching of academic disciplines among teams, and there was no interinstitutional communication about team selections. These issues seemed to have no relevance.

The plan called for the three teams to assemble once on each campus during the year: the first time in October, the second in January, and the third in March. The visits lasted three days and were carefully scheduled with consideration to local calendars and other factors. To prevent the first campus visit from becoming a get-acquainted session, an orientation meeting was deemed advisable. This brief session was planned, therefore, as the first of four meetings for the year. The orientation was held at a neutral site — a college or university campus convenient to all teams — during late summer. The design of the orientation program promotes general understanding about the three institutions and fosters the beginning of new friendships. As a consequence, the first campus visit in October can begin with the greeting of "old friends" and the sense of having been there before. No start-up time is required.

The orientation program is necessarily conducted by senior administrators who accompany the teams to the neutral site. Beyond giving a broad view of the institution, which ordinarily they alone may have, the administrators serve the vital function of generating faculty interest by their involvement in the program and their commitment to its success. Nonetheless, the program is a faculty effort, and the administrators must begin to withdraw as the orientation proceeds, as teams begin building interest in one another, and as the first host launches preparations for the October visit. The structure of the orientation program allows administrators to assume this diminished role because the middle third of the orientation is devoted to small-group dynamics that involve faculty members in an exchange of mutual and individual concerns relevant to the pending visits. Once the orientation session is concluded, the full burden of responsibility shifts to the teams and their captains. Acceptance of that responsibility by the faculty must be accompanied by assurance of support and a commitment to participate on the part of the senior administrators.

Each of the campus visits lasts for approximately three days. In that interval there are planned features, opportunities for informal rap sessions, and individual conferences. Advance planning by the host team permits efficient use of the time and guarantees a full schedule, yet there is a stated principle that each visitor may pursue his or her own interests regardless of the planned agenda. The importance of social interactions and pleasures should not be ignored.

The planned features can include an overview of the host institution by its president. It is best for the president to give the overview extemporaneously in response to questions prepared in advance by the host team; this feature should come early in the visit. Time can be devoted to a treatment of social programs, institutes, and unique projects. Free discussion time with students is highly desirable, as is time with individual faculty members or groups. Special topics that seem always to command general interest include faculty development, shared governance, curriculum planning, plans for exigencies, and support for research. There are many specialized targets of inquiry: syllabus design, teaching techniques, basic skill deficiencies among students, research techniques, and a host of other issues.

Early on, ten objectives were set for the exchange program; the success of a visit or series of visits can be measured against them:

- To expand understanding of the home institution by the opportunity of a close study of other institutions
- To discover some new solutions to old problems
- To discover some old solutions to new problems
- To discover some new and different uses of institutional resources, both human and physical
- To discover something about the differences in the organization and decision-making processes among institutions and why there may be a need for such differences
- To gain a larger understanding of how pervasive the problems of education are—how permanent they seem to be and how tentative or temporary the solutions seem to be
- To learn enough about the broad issues of university management to permit a better formulation of what should be expected at the home institution
- To gain some knowledge of how institutions may stand alone or in symbiosis with the world about them, and why they choose to be as they are
- To effect some personal bonds of friendship which may engender individual professional and institutional relationships
- To sustain personal gratification via new insights and renewed enthusiasm for the central task of educating students.

The faculty exchange program is directed at the individual professor. While there is hope that other faculty members will gain vicariously from the exchanges—and indeed they do—there should be no expectation of a quick or even noticeable effect upon the general academic community. The goal is individual development. There is no hidden agenda except, of course, improved instruction for future students.

At the end of each day of a visit, all team members—even the hosts—are asked to make entries in a journal. The journal is a personal written record of what was learned and how that learning occurred.

The preparation of a journal is important because it helps team members remember all that is worth remembering. The journals can be useful in other ways as well; the team members can mine them for information and recommendations to the administration, the faculty senate, or student government. The journals can have other values, as will be discussed later.

The teams meet four times during the year. Team members use these occasions to get new ideas or refine ideas previously presented. A single occasion together in any place would readily lead to the dissemination of ideas and the spreading of good will, but the recurrence of seasons together encourages the further consideration of those ideas. From the journals kept in early visits, team members may retrieve points that deserve further discussion or refinement. In the pilot project, the journals were examined by an outside agency to test the efficacy of the exchange program.

Once the program is operational and the orientation concluded, the administrators are removed from active leadership, and the faculty participants must develop knowledge of their own institution as they prepare for the visitors. In the process, faculty gain knowledge about many aspects of their institutions — the corporate nature of the institution, the independent and interdependent functioning of its units, and even the existence of previously unknown buildings and services. Operations of the home campus are now seen through the eyes of the expected visitors rather than in the narrow view so easily adopted at home. The informed host will be less inclined to dispense hearsay as fact and will favor instead objective fact. This knowledge enhances appreciation of the home institution and improves communication with the home administrators.

The general learning that occurs in the Revolving Faculty Exchange Program combined with the specialized learning about curriculum and teaching have been salutary experiences for the faculty members involved. Novel ideas work in unique ways to affect the quality of teaching, while the larger comprehension of university operations tends to reduce anxiety. Communications with administrators seem easier and less threatening.

In the preparation for and the conduct of the exchange program, faculty members often gain a new sense of pride in the home institution. Having at once the opportunity of hosting visitors to the campus and of making direct comparisons with other universities fosters a pride in their institution greater than is possible in the isolation of one campus. An awareness of the universal nature of educational problems is part of an informed view about problem solving and relieves some of the tensions that work against effective teaching and wise counseling of students.

The brevity of each visit in the exchange program may suggest inadequate opportunity for substantive learning. Indeed, the time might be too limited were it not for the keynote of the exchanges — candor. When faculty and administrators alike commit themselves to the program, there is an implicit pledge of candor; where this virtue exists, it compensates for the shortage of time. Further, the high degree of independence of the visitors is a fine alternative to learning about universities through climbing organizational ladders.

Candor is brought about not only by the commitment of the university community but also through the special conditions imposed on the three-institution network. It is wise to choose three colleges or universities whose distance from each other guarantees a minimum of competition for students or jobs. Obviously, the institutions cannot be financed from the same pocketbook, else there would be reluctance to reveal state secrets. Two other important selection criteria are the nature of governance and the degree level. Thus all three should be public or all independent; all should be doctoral granting institutions or all degree levels below the doctorate. Institution size appears to be of no consequence.

Senior administrators must be involved in forming a network. The president or chancellor is of primary importance to the program, for without his or her support and interest the program will either abort or take on a completely different meaning. It is the president who pledges the essential candor and openness of the university, and the president must back the pledge by example. Similarly, it is the president who commits the university and its support structure by budgetary allocation.

Senior administrators have responsibilities for the institution as a whole. For this reason they can bring the program into being, whereas faculty members may not with any facility. The object of the program is the immersion of hosting and visiting faculty in the life of the university, and it is vital that no area (save the treasury) be closed to them. That openness cannot be gained by faculty alone.

Were the faculty members granted the right and responsibility for devising their own faculty exchange program, it is almost inevitable that they would elect to bring visiting scholars for seminars and lectures. There is great enrichment in these kinds of visits, but the effects on attitudes are likely to be negligible. The stimulation is directed to scholarship and obliquely to teaching but not at all to the work environment or the nature of the university. Significantly, as the pilot Revolving Faculty Exchange Program was being planned, the idea of visitors giving lectures or seminars was considered to be extraneous to the general purpose of the program.

A natural question about the exchange program is cost. The happy answer is very little — less than one-half the cost of one sabbatical leave for one person. The host institution assumes the responsibility for food and housing during the visit, and the visitors provide their own transportation. Costs for the orientation program are held to a minimum when the neutral site is the campus of a college or university willing to make space available at little cost. Obviously, there are no honoraria or related charges.

Can the benefits of the exchange program be measured? The answer is negative if the measures must include papers published or grant applications authorized. It is doubtful that any changes in grade distributions can be discerned. The voluntary testimony of participants, however, together with the aura of newfound enthusiasm, convey strong impressions of success. No participant has spoken negatively about the experience, and the majority have been high in praise, even to the extent of recruiting into the next team some who "obviously need this kind of experience." On concluding its year, the team plays a role in selecting the group for the next year. Where there was the intent to explore a curriculum or pedagogical issue, the relations have not ended with the conclusion of the year-long program. Oral and written communications have been sustained.

Latent talents of leadership materialize in the unusual milieu of the exchange program, and there are examples of formerly reticent faculty members assuming responsible roles in faculty governance and curriculum design. At least one faculty member with a somewhat jaundiced view about administration decided at the end of his year to seek an administrative post. These changes redound to the benefit of the students.

The exchange program has not been without direct benefit to the senior administrators. From the beginning of the pilot program, during which the administrators announced their intent to participate only when asked, there has been faculty encouragement for participation by administrators. Hence, on every campus visit, there have been senior officers along, who normally choose to pursue agendas of their own. Aside from the warm personal relationships that evolve both intramurally and among their counterparts in other colleges, there has been an exchange of ideas in organization and program. The administrators have endeavored to stand clear of the planning and the major activities of the exchanges, yet it is noteworthy that the administrative participants seem to reinforce the vital ingredient of candor.

The pilot network ran for two years. Because there are new teams each year, the network could have been extended beyond that time, but the consensus was to terminate the original and form new networks. Probably there is psychological value in the introduction of new institutions, together with the fact that the experience of each network member can guide the formation of a new network.

In principle, the Revolving Faculty Exchange Program can go on indefinitely, the requisites being nothing more than administrative support and faculty willingness. Numerous variations on the plan are possible, and some have been tried successfully. In the 1980–81 academic year, through the auspices of the Resource Center for Planned Change, thirty colleges and universities in ten groups of three each are participating in exchanges similar to those described in this chapter. While the program affects only a limited number of faculty each year and is not a panacea for the great problems of education, it is a positive step toward the improvement of teaching quality. The program proves that staff development is possible without a special office or bureau or the commitment of large sums of money.

Charles B. Vail is president of Winthrop College in South Carolina. He has served on the Advisory Committee of the Resource Center for Planned Change and is a member of the Board of Directors of the American Association of State Colleges and Universities.

Presidents and academic vice-presidents symbolize and are
concerned with university-wide academic interests. Thus
they are vital to developing the consensus and climate
through which teaching goals are realized.

Concluding Comments

Alan E. Guskin

The chapters in this sourcebook have portrayed a number of programs,
planning activities, and styles of administration dedicated to the facilitation of quality teaching. The primary purpose of these chapters is to
provide the reader with an analysis and examples of how administrators influence the teaching and learning process by creating organizational environments within which faculty members can be creative
teachers.

The case studies represent examples of how administrators relate
to teaching. In the academic planning process taking place at SUNY
College at Potsdam, and at nine other state colleges and universities
throughout the country, the faculty have embarked on a rather elaborate project to analyze and possibly rethink the ways in which students
learn. Similarly, on the many campuses that have used the Futures
Creating Paradigm, faculty and staff have embarked on university-
wide efforts that affect the teaching/learning process. Surely faculty
could initiate some of these efforts on their own; but the reality is that
such a process is not initiated without strong, persuasive, and persis-
tent administrative leadership. Such leadership is required to assure
faculty members that their endeavor is an important institutional prior-

ity. This is concretized in the allocation of resources to the planning process and any subsequent implementation efforts.

However, there is a more important issue: it is the president and academic vice-president who symbolize and are concerned with university-wide academic interests. Faculty members, like all individuals in complex organizations, look to such leaders to legitimize broad institutional concerns. Faculty members are necessarily concerned with their particular disciplines and even subdisciplines. They are also highly individualistic in their endeavors—their teaching is carried out alone with students; their scholarship is often a highly personal venture.

The president and academic vice-president are, therefore, in an important position to facilitate the development of university-wide planning processes. Their success depends greatly on the manner or style with which they relate to members of the planning group and the faculty generally. As Ratner emphasizes, the effective chief academic officer is a persuader rather than one who commands; he or she enters into dialogue with colleagues rather than presents fully elucidated plans. The role of the academic officer is to develop a consensus that allows the faculty and administration to work together for common objectives; it is to create an organizational environment in which faculty and staff feel effective and competent and, therefore, are responsive to institution-wide concerns critical to the future of the university. This seems to have happened at Potsdam and has led to a very creative endeavor.

The academic planning process at Potsdam affords an opportunity for faculty to discuss their intellectual and educational aspirations openly with their colleagues—a rare experience at most universities. The intellectual vitality of those directly involved in the coordinating committee and all those who were affected by them was considerably enhanced by the academic planning process. This same rare experience of in-depth discussions of educational issues is also reported by Greenebaum in the planning that led to the creation of the Collegiate Skills Program.

The very nature of the enterprises at Potsdam and the University of Wisconsin–Parkside and some of the institutions involved in the Futures Creating Paradigm emphasizes the critical role that faculty members play in the life of the university. The planning process at the institutional level almost always clarifies who has influence—and both faculty and staff rarely miss the message in the nature of participation in this process.

Not all administrative facilitation of quality teaching is a result of university-wide planning processes. The example of how a small program and a simple idea can have substantial impact on individual faculty members, and through them their colleagues, is seen in the chapter on the Revolving Faculty Exchange Program. An idea conceived by Vail, president of Winthrop College, tested out with his own and two other institutions involving about six or seven faculty members on each campus, has now spread to over thirty universities throughout the country. Through these exchanges literally hundreds of faculty members are learning how other universities operate, learning about the creative aspects of their own campuses and, through all of this, gaining a renewed sense of pride in their own institutions.

An important thread that runs through the exchange program, the Futures Creating Paradigm, and the Academic Program Evaluation Project (APEP) is the role of the Resource Center for Planned Change. A function of the American Association of State Colleges and Universities, composed of over 340 institutions, the center works collaboratively with academic vice-presidents to create an interest in planning. Out of these efforts emerged the planning paradigm, APEP, and the dissemination of the faculty exchange projects reported in this sourcebook. As is seen in the chapter on Potsdam, the Resource Center played an extremely favorable role in facilitating the planning process there. It should be emphasized that both the president and academic vice-president at Potsdam are active members of the Center, as is Charles Vail of Winthrop College.

In many ways, the Resource Center is a unique venture in stimulating academic officers, and often their presidents, to think about the teaching and learning needs of their faculty and students and to utilize one or another planning strategy to enhance the quality and effectiveness of these matters on their campuses. Often the dissemination of new strategies or programs occurs because academic officers talk to each other in a noncompetitive, off-campus situation; sometimes a planning effort is recognized as important for the campus, and the academic officer, having heard about the Resource Center, seeks aid from the staff; on still other occasions the staff members of the center, having developed a series of regional and national seminars with academic officers around a specific issue (for example, academic program evaluation), write a proposal for funding of the project that evolved from the discussions and then request colleges and universities to participate; and on fewer occasions, a creative president, having conceived a program that has implications for other campuses, asks the staff of the center to help with its design and eventual dissemination (for example, revolving faculty exchange). For the colleges and universities involved, the Resource Center is an important vehicle for program planning.

As we move into the difficult days of the 1980s, such a center will become even more important in providing stimulation and guidance to beleaguered university administrators on how to remain creative and concerned with educational issues during periods of retrenchment. The hope is that through such activity the Resource Center will enable universities to have more choices than those conceived of by the CUNY colleges in the 1970s and dealt with by Ratner in his sensitive discussion of the dilemma he and his colleagues faced in New York.

Besides university-wide planning dealing with curricular issues, facilitating quality teaching is dependent on the ability of students to learn and the availability of resources to support the teaching effort. Faculty members want to feel as sense of ownership in their university, but for this to have meaning for their teaching, there must be a pride in the quality of what they offer their students. In this regard, the espousal of quality and the concrete manifestation of this value in programs that overtly support the maintenance of academic standards is important. The chapter on collegiate skills at the University of Wisconsin–Parkside gives an example of such a program. The faculty and administration collaborated in the effort to create and implement this program, each providing the resources available to them. The result at Parkside has been upgraded student skills, greater confidence by faculty that they can maintain appropriate academic standards, and considerable pride in the university because it is concerned with quality and has received national and state recognition for its work.

The chapter on the two teaching libraries gives an example of how administrators facilitate the teaching process by supporting faculty and students in the learning process. By reordering priorities, the directors of these two libraries were able to redirect the efforts of their staffs without any increase in financial support to their units.

Teaching and learning are the primary functions of almost all universities. Yet the interaction between the faculty and students is carried out in a rather isolated manner in a classroom, behind closed doors, out of view of everyone except the participants. Because of this, it is easy to think that the only manner in which this interaction can be enhanced is by increasing the skills of the teacher. Of course, this is important but it is not the only means for increasing the quality of the teaching and learning process. Although the teacher and student are isolated in the classroom, they are also active participants in a complex institution and are directly affected by the nature of the organizational environment in which they work. If the quality of life that faculty members experience at a university is less than desirable, this fact will be reflected in the way they feel about working at the campus, about their colleagues, and about their students. On the other hand, if faculty members feel good about themselves personally and professionally—if they feel a sense of intellectual vitality, a sense of ownership, a sense of pride, a sense of security—and believe that students have the capability to meet appropriate academic standards and utilize available educational resources, then they will be better teachers.

It is the main point of this sourcebook that senior university administrators play a vital role in creating the type of organizational environments that lead to a desirable quality of life for faculty members. Enhanced quality of life in turn positively affects their teaching. If this is so, then it is important for administrators to strive to develop creative organizational environments. We have tried to conceptualize what this means and give some practical examples of it throughout this sourcebook.

Alan E. Guskin, a social psychologist, has been chancellor of the University of Wisconsin–Parkside for the last six years. Previously, he served as provost and acting president of Clark University in Worcester, Massachusetts. A professor of education, he remains active as a teacher, scholar, and consultant, particularly in the areas of university leadership and organizational change in educational institutions. He has served as chairman of the Advisory Committee of the Resource Center for Planned Change and is a member of the Board of Directors of the American Association of State Colleges and Universities.

The purpose and functions of the Resource Center
for Planned Change are presented in this
final chapter.

Further Resources:
The Resource Center
for Planned Change

Marina Buhler-Miko

Throughout this sourcebook readers will notice references to the Resource
Center for Planned Change of the American Association of State Colleges and Universities (AASCU). A number of the programs described
by the authors grew out of the work of the Resource Center; the Academic Program Evaluation Project at SUNY College at Potsdam is a
part of the Resource Center's APEP Project; the Revolving Faculty
Exchange Program was developed by the president of Winthrop College in cooperation with the Resource Center, and the center continues
to link up institutions for the purpose of this exchange; the Futures
Creating Paradigm is a planning model developed by the Resource
Center; even Guskin's own analysis of leadership styles was first presented to the Resource Center's Summer Institute on leadership for
academic vice-presidents. It is, therefore, important to describe the
purpose and functioning of the Resource Center for Planned Change.

The Resource Center for Planned Change is designed to help AASCU institutions in their efforts to plan for the future. To understand the Resource Center one has to go back to the early 1970s and the work of the National Commission on the Future of State Colleges, chaired by Senator Wayne L. Morse. This commission seriously considered the future of those state colleges and universities that had emerged from teachers' colleges into comprehensive institutions and directed its concern at the appropriate role and scope of these institutions in the future. The subsequent report of this commission suggests that serious attention be given to the emerging role and scope of this valuable and viable section of American higher education and that such attention not be in the form of "directives from on high," but in new roles developed by the campuses themselves.

To the vice-chairman, President Albert W. Brown of SUNY College at Brockport, and to committee member President Paul Romberg of San Francisco State University must go the credit for recognizing, when the commission and its campus-action team reports were completed, that the job of AASCU in assisting its institutions to identify future purposes, scope, and roles was far from over. In 1974, these presidents plus the executive director of AASCU, Allan Ostar, proposed to the W. K. Kellogg Foundation that the work of the Commission be carried on by a center located within AASCU's national offices. In the summer of 1975, the Resource Center for Planned Change was created along with an Advisory Committee of presidents and chancellors drawn from the AASCU membership under the chairmanship of Paul Romberg. It was supported by a substantial grant from the W. K. Kellogg Foundation. The first director of the Resource Center was Kent Alm, presently commissioner of higher education in North Dakota.

The need for a Resource Center continued to grow and, because of the center's success in assisting state colleges and universities to plan for their futures, the membership of AASCU voted in 1978 to make the Resource Center a permanent arm of the association. It stands today as a part of AASCU, supported by the membership as a planning and development resource for all AASCU institutions.

The Resource Center for Planned Change acts as a catalyst and source of new ideas for senior academic officers in AASCU institutions in their efforts to plan for the future. The center's approaches to planning are designed to assist AASCU institutions and reflect an understanding of the needs of college and university communities today. Through the programs for senior academic administrators, comprehensive approaches to institutional planning, and a variety of support services, the center attempts to respond to the current needs of AASCU institutions as well as act as an agent in their longer-term growth and development.

The Center Associates Program

Much of the center's success rests on the development of a network of center associates — senior academic officers from state colleges and universities. Presidents and chancellors of AASCU institutions have designated their senior academic officers to serve as center associates. There are now more than 300 center associates in the network, each of whom has a major responsibility for the academic future of their campuses. Center associates advise the center on issues of concern, work with the center to develop planning approaches to these problems, and, hopefully, put into practice on their campuses processes that will effect academic change and improvement.

The center associates meet regularly in a sequence of seminars. In the fall of each year the center holds three-day regional seminars in the four regions of the United States. In the spring, the center holds a three-day national seminar, which enables center associates from all over the country to work together. Each summer the center holds a five-day summer institute for up to thirty center associates. This is an intensive seminar that gives center associates the opportunity to pull together the ideas developed over the course of a year's worth of seminars and task force meetings on a particular topic.

Each year a topic of major concern is chosen for examination through this sequence of seminars. Ideas for planning and change emerge from the regional meetings. The Resource Center and its staff review the ideas, sometimes with additional help from center associates or outside consultants in fields such as the social sciences, business and management, and other research areas of academic expertise. The topic, with the outline of a possible approach and guidelines for implementation, is taken to the national seminar for further work and exploration by the center associates. The resultant planning approach is further refined and developed at the center's summer institute. Topics examined have included the changing nature of academic affairs, values and the undergraduate curriculum, and effective resource allocation.

What ultimately emerges from the center associates program is a support network of senior academic officers who understand the issues confronting them more fully because they have spent time working on them and on the planning approaches together.

Planning Approaches

The Center's approaches to planning are based on certain key ideas about how planning should be conducted in higher educational institutions, ideas that have developed over the years through the interaction with the center associates and their institutions.

The leadership of colleges and universities can plan their future deliberately. Although many seem to believe that higher education institutions should not or cannot plan, the Resource Center's approach is that administrators must be involved actively in planning the future of their institution. Administrators must do this carefully and deliberately, with the welfare of their institutions and students in mind.

For planning to be meaningful, it must be participatory. Planning must involve faculty and administrators working together and reaching consensus on the plans that are developed. Further, in order for plans to be more than just rhetoric, they need to be developed by the faculty and administrators of a particular institution rather than by a state, regional, or national group.

Planning must be anticipatory. Planning should try to anticipate the future with the best means available and direct the individual college or university toward that future. The approach of the Resource Center is that data and technology cannot be as effective in anticipating the future as well-informed people working together. The center respects and relies on the ability of college and university faculty and administrators to anticipate their own future directions.

Effective planning must be a conceptual process carried out at a variety of levels. Substantive plans must be created for the new programs of any institution. Strategic and feasibility plans must be created to explain how such programs will be implemented, what decisions have to be made, and who is going to run the programs. In developing implementation strategies, emphasis is placed on gaining the support of key decision makers who must ultimately approve the plans. Further, the normative and value concerns of the faculty and staff of any institution must inform the planning process. Planners must be willing to take the time to consider basic value differences and work toward a new consensus that does not ignore but rather includes the important, time-honored values of education.

Resource Center Outcomes

These key ideas support the development of planning paradigms, or models, by senior academic officers working together for the purpose of designing approaches they can use on their own campuses. Outcomes of the Resource Center's planning approaches include the following:

Futures Creating Paradigm. This first paradigm, described in Chapter Three, is an approach to long-range planning for colleges and universities designed by the center and its associates in 1976-77. The ten-stage process of the paradigm explores the relationships of societal change to all sectors of an institution and indicates how those future conditions relate to educational policy development and curriculum design. The Futures Creating Paradigm is presently being used by many colleges and universities all over the United States.

Academic Program Evaluation Paradigm. This second paradigm, described in Chapter Four, was developed through the efforts of center staff and associates in 1977-78. The paradigm is an institutional process to define and evaluate the key cross-disciplinary thinking skills — communication, analysis, synthesis, quantification, and valuing — so that institutions may identify and improve the quality of the baccalaureate programs. Through the Academic Program Evaluation Project (APEP), supported in part by a grant from the Fund for the Improvement of Postsecondary Education, the five-stage process of the paradigm is now being implemented by ten AASCU institutions, where more than 250 faculty members are involved in its use.

The Changing Nature of Academic Affairs and Team Process Leadership. The third approach to planning was developed and worked on during 1978-79. It provides a useful analysis of the activities and responsibilities under the purview of academic affairs today. It also develops the concept of team process leadership, described in Chapter One, whereby the more effective leader builds a team approach. It is through this team that the expansion of his or her leadership takes place. Finally, it explains some of the new developments currently being tried in organizational management.

Ethics and Valuing and the Undergraduate Curriculum. The center and its associates worked on this approach in 1979-80. This effort focused on university mission statements written in outcome form, used the latest research in intellectual and ethical development of students, and sought out the best strategies for working with curriculum committees. In the summer institute, center associates worked on two ideas: (1) the implementation of "communities of scale" on our campuses, which would be set up to enable students and faculty to deal with the ethical and value dimension of education; and (2) the use of values and ethics in university and college leadership decision making. The concepts developed are currently being pulled together by center staff for publication in the near future. Also under consideration is a small grant to work with senior academic officers on ethical and value analysis and training for decision making on a university-wide basis.

Revolving Institutional Exchange Program. This unique and ongoing program of the Center, described in Chapter Seven, provides the opportunity for faculty and administrators of AASCU institutions to team up and visit each other. The program stimulates institutional self-study and exploration and thereby improves faculty understanding of administrative issues, increases everyone's knowledge about and pride in their institution, and often eases people's readiness to consider change. Presently, thirty universities are involved in exchanges.

Support Services

In addition to the outcomes of the planning approaches developed by center staff and associates and the resulting services made available to AASCU institutions, the Resource Center is also engaged in a number of services designed to keep center associates informed on matters related to long-term institutional planning.

Program Resource Bank. This service, currently being developed by the center, will identify and make available to center associates ideas, programs, and people that will be helpful to AASCU institutions faced with critical problems brought about by change; examples of such are remedial/developmental program efforts, student retention activities, and academic program quality improvement. The service provides an opportunity for institutions, through their center associates, to work together and share knowledge for individual campus improvement.

On-Campus Consulting. As assisting agency to some AASCU institutions in their Education Department Title III (Developing Universities) projects as well as by individual campus request, Center staff are available for on-campus consulting activities relating to specific institutional planning problems, the use of the Futures Creating Paradigm, and the implementation of the Academic Program Evaluation Project at institutions beyond those involved in the pilot project.

Trend Analysis. The Trend Analysis Service, which is just starting for Title III colleges and universities working on futures planning, will provide a methodology for individual campus trend research, thus assisting institutions and their faculties as they research their own local and regional trends. The service will also provide a source for ascertaining alternative trends in key areas drawn from available national, international, and regional data.

Publications. *Alternatives,* the Center's principal periodical publication, reports and explains the topics and planning approaches discussed in the cycle of center associate meetings. This newsletter/journal, containing the thinking of center associates, national experts, and center staff, is a forum for substantive issues of academic change and improvement. In addition, the Resource Center has published *A Futures Creating Paradigm,* is soon to publish *The Academic Program Evaluation Paradigm* and a guide on the Revolving Institutional Exchange Program. Finally, the *Center Associates Directory* facilitates the work of the network for senior academic officers on AASCU campuses.

All the efforts of the Resource Center are focused on the improvement of the more than 340 colleges and universities that are members of AASCU. The seminars and the network of center associates provide a type of leadership training that is desired by senior academic administrators. The center's approaches to planning assist AASCU institutions as they work to plan for the future. Through its programs and services, center associates receive not only information on issues and procedures but a fuller understanding of the issues and approaches available to them. In summary, the Resource Center for Planned Change is a resource responding to current and specific needs of this nation's state colleges and universities and acting as a catalyst in their continuing growth and development.

*Marina Buhler-Miko is the director of the
Resource Center for Planned Change.*

Index

F

Faculty: academic planning role of, 48–49; and curricular development, 21; development centers for, 19–20; in dialogue on values, 17–24; effect of library skills program on, 74–75; exchange program for, 79–87; intellectual vitality in, 2, 6–7, 11, 13; knowledge of other institutions by, 6, 79–87; as maypole dancers, 27; and mobility, 21–22, 80; ownership by, 2, 3–5, 13; pride by, 2, 5–6, 12, 13, 54, 64–65, 84–85; quality of life for, 2–7, 13, 93; and rewards system, 20; security of, 2–3, 8, 10, 12, 13; and skills program, 60–61, 63–65; and teaching-research relationship, 19–20
Farber, E. I., 70, 71, 75, 76, 77
Feasibility, and futures planning, 37
Fiscal resources: and academic administrators, 22–23; and faculty security, 3
Foresight, and futures planning, 37
Fund for the Improvement of Postsecondary Education (FIPSE), 42, 45, 99
Futures, alternative, and futures planning, 36–37
Futures Creating Paradigm, 89, 90, 91; assumptions of, 32; origins of, 29–32; and participation, 31; and policy plan, 37–38; process and stages of, 33–37; and Resource Center for Planned Change, 25, 26, 95, 99, 100–101
Futures Planning, and community building, 25–39

G

Greenebaum, B., 15, 53–65, 90
Gruber, J., 74, 77
Gruskin, S., 31
Guskin, A. E., vii–x, 1–15, 27, 56, 60, 65, 68–69, 78, 89–93, 95

H

Harder, S., 65
Harvard University, general education program at, 59
Harvey, W. H., 74–75, 78
Hegarty, T. J., 14, 41–52

Higher education: constraints in, 17–18, 27, 79–80; futures planning and sense of community in, 25–39

I

Influence, authority related to, 11
Intellectual vitality: in academic administrators, 24; in faculty, 2, 6–7, 11, 13

K

Karter, S., 78
Kellogg Foundation, W. K., 29–30, 96
Kennedy, J. R., Jr., 71, 78
Kirk, T. J., 71, 78
Kolka, J. W., 65

L

Last, E., 65
Leadership, conceptual analysis scarce on, vii–viii, 1. See also Administrators
Lehman College, retrenchment at, 14. See also City University of New York
Lenehan, W. L., 65
Levine, A., 27–28, 39
Library: and administrators, 76–77; bibliographic instruction program of, 69, 71, 72–73; potential of, 67–68; and quality teaching, 67–68; and teaching, 73–75; teaching type of, 68–69

M

McGahan, S. L., 65
Maine, University of, at Machias, Futures Creating Paradigm at, 31–32
Mayville State College, Futures Creating Paradigm at, 31
Middle States Association of Schools and Colleges, and outcomes assessment, 45
Morse, W. L., 96
Myrbo, C. L., 65

N

National Commission on the Future of State Colleges, 96
Nebraska-Omaha, University of, Academic Program Evaluation Project at, 43

New Directions Quarterly Sourcebooks

New Directions for Teaching and Learning is one of several distinct series of quarterly sourcebooks published by Jossey-Bass. The sourcebooks in each series are designed to serve both as *convenient compendiums* of the latest knowledge and practical experience on their topics and as *long-life reference tools.*

One-year, four-sourcebook subscriptions for each series cost $18 for individuals (when paid by personal check) and $30 for institutions, libraries, and agencies. Single copies of earlier sourcebooks are available at $6.95 each *prepaid* (or $7.95 each when *billed*).

A complete listing is given below of current and past sourcebooks in the *New Directions for Teaching and Learning* series. The titles and editors-in-chief of the other series are also listed. To subscribe, or to receive further information, write: New Directions Subscriptions, Jossey-Bass Inc., Publishers, 433 California Street, San Francisco, California 94104.

New Directions for Teaching and Learning
Kenneth E. Eble and John F. Noonan, Editors-in-Chief
1980:   1. *Improving Teaching Styles,* Kenneth E. Eble
        2. *Learning, Cognition, and College Teaching,*
           Wilbert J. McKeachie
        3. *Fostering Critical Thinking,* Robert E. Young
        4. *Learning About Teaching,* John F. Noonan

New Directions for Child Development
William Damon, Editor-in-Chief

New Directions for College Learning Assistance
Kurt V. Lauridsen, Editor-in-Chief

New Directions for Community Colleges
Arthur M. Cohen, Editor-in-Chief
Florence B. Brawer, Associate Editor

New Directions for Continuing Education
Alan B. Knox, Editor-in-Chief

New Directions for Exceptional Children
James J. Gallagher, Editor-in-Chief

New Directions for Experiential Learning
Pamela J. Tate, Editor-in-Chief
Morris T. Keeton, Consulting Editor

New Directions for Higher Education
JB Lon Hefferlin, Editor-in-Chief

New Directions for Institutional Advancement
A. Westley Rowland, Editor-in-Chief

New Directions for Institutional Research
Marvin W. Peterson, Editor-in-Chief

New Directions for Mental Health Services
H. Richard Lamb, Editor-in-Chief

New Directions for Methodology of Social and Behavioral Science
Donald W. Fiske, Editor-in-Chief

New Directions for Program Evaluation
Scarvia B. Anderson, Editor-in-Chief

New Directions for Student Services
Ursula Delworth and Gary R. Hanson, Editors-in-Chief

New Directions for Testing and Measurement
William B. Schrader, Editor-in-Chief